Valiant Vel

VEL PHILLIPS and the Fight for Fairness and Equality

Jerrianne Hayslett

Illustrations by **Aaron Boyd** | Afterword by **Michael Phillips**

WISCONSIN HISTORICAL SOCIETY PRESS

Published by the Wisconsin Historical Society Press
Publishers since 1855

The Wisconsin Historical Society helps people connect to the past by collecting, preserving, and sharing stories. Founded in 1846, the Society is one of the nation's finest historical institutions.
Join the Wisconsin Historical Society: wisconsinhistory.org/membership

Text © 2025 by Jerrianne Hayslett. Cover and interior illustrations © 2024 by Aaron Boyd.

Publication of this book was made possible in part by a grant from the D.C. Everest fellowship fund.

For permission to reuse material from *Valiant Vel* (ISBN 978-1-9766-0043-2; e-book ISBN 978-1-9766-0044-9), please access www.copyright.com or contact the Copyright Clearance Center, Inc. (CCC), 222 Rosewood Drive, Danvers, MA 01923, 978-750-8400. CCC is a not-for-profit organization that provides licenses and registration for a variety of users.

Photographs identified with WHi or WHS are from the Society's collections; address requests to reproduce these photos to the Visual Materials Archivist at the Wisconsin Historical Society, 816 State Street, Madison, WI 53706.

Front cover photograph: WHi image ID 97930
Back cover photograph, WHi image ID 119125; brochure, WHi image ID 120192

Printed in Wisconsin, USA
Designed by Brian Donahue / bedesign, inc.

29 28 27 26 25   1 2 3 4 5

Library of Congress Cataloging-in-Publication Data available.

♾ The paper used in this publication meets the minimum requirements of the American National Standard for Information Sciences—Permanence of Paper for Printed Library Materials, ANSI Z39.48-1992.

This biography of Vel Phillips is dedicated to her husband, Warren Dale Phillips, who was her chief supporter, strategist, anchor, influencer, and counsel. While Vel engaged in public service, Dale kept their family, the household, and their Phillips & Phillips law firm running. He partnered with her in every aspect of their lives and was her best friend.

Table of Contents

Chapter 1: The Speech Contest — 1

Chapter 2: Velvalea Speaks Up — 5

Chapter 3: "I Want to Be a Lawyer" — 12

Chapter 4: Law School and a Lifelong Partnership — 18

Chapter 5: Bronzeville — 22

Chapter 6: Impossible Odds — 30

Chapter 7: Madam Alderman — 36

Chapter 8: Vel's Fight for Fair Housing Begins — 44

Chapter 9: Obstacles and Opposition — 48

Chapter 10: The NAACP Youth Council Joins the Fight — 57

Chapter 11: Marching for Fairness and Equality — 64

Chapter 12: These Marchers Won't Back Down — 74

Chapter 13: "Nobody Is Free Until Everybody Is Free" — 80

Chapter 14: "This Is My Work" — 83

Chapter 15: Wanted: Courage   88

Chapter 16: Two Hundred Dangerous Days   93

Chapter 17: A Fair Housing Ordinance at Last   98

Chapter 18: "Victory Is Always Possible"   104

Epilogue   111

Afterword   116

Author's Note   118

Acknowledgments   120

Glossary   122

Bibliography   125

Source Notes   127

Index   134

Image Credits   141

Chapter 1

The Speech Contest

Velvalea Rodgers didn't mean to start a protest. She just wanted to participate in a high school speech contest. She thought that would be good experience for an aspiring lawyer like herself.

Participating in the contest turned out to be a valuable experience, but not in the way she had expected.

It was 1939. The United States was recovering from the decade-long Great Depression and was a little more than two years away from entering World War II. Velvalea was in her junior year at North Division High School in Milwaukee, Wisconsin. She told the school's **forensics** teacher, Helen Muellenschlader, the kind of speech she wanted to give in North Division's annual speech contest. As the forensics teacher, Miss Muellenschlader conducted the contest.

Velvalea Rodgers's high school yearbook picture

According to the contest rules, participants could either choose from Miss Muellenschlader's collection of prepared essays or write their own speech on a topic she approved. The prepared essays were divided into three categories: serious narrative, humorous narrative, and **oratory**. Whether participants chose an essay from Miss Muellenschlader's collection or wrote their own, they had to memorize it and present it as a speech without using notes.

When Velvalea asked Miss Muellenschlader for an oratory essay, the teacher said they were all checked out. Since students could keep an essay for only three weeks, Velvalea waited then asked again. Sorry, the teacher said, her face a stern mask. None had been returned. Velvalea asked again every week or so. Every time, Miss Muellenschlader had no oratory essay to give her.

Velvalea shared her frustrations with another teacher, Agnes Roberts. She and Miss Roberts got along well and Velvalea trusted her. Miss Roberts recalled an oratory essay Velvalea had written for a non-school contest the previous summer. She suggested Velvalea enter that essay in the forensics competition. Titled "They Shall Not Pass," the essay dealt with difficulties Black Americans faced when they tried to achieve success in life, to live where they wanted to, to attend the schools they wanted to, to get good jobs, and to be treated fairly.

Velvalea wavered. Would Miss Muellenschlader approve her essay? Well, she wouldn't know unless she asked. But when she told the forensics teacher what she wanted to do and asked if she would approve her essay, Miss Muellenschlader became irritated. She told Velvalea to select a humorous essay from her collection instead.

"Now, young lady," the teacher said, peering at Velvalea through her wire-rimmed glasses, "you should choose something that fits your people, and that certainly would not be a serious oration. Your people are very good at comedy." The movie character Buckwheat was a good example, she said. Buckwheat was the stereotype of a little Black kid in the *Our Gang* movies, which were popular at the time. "I think one of the humorous declamations [speeches] would work out just fine."

Why was the teacher treating her like that? Velvalea knew she could never do anything humorous, much less comedic. Other contest participants were giving oratory speeches. Why couldn't she give her own? As one of North Division's few Black students, Velvalea chafed against the racial stereotype her teacher had used to stop her from presenting the speech she wanted to.

Velvalea tried to hide her outrage. But what could she do?

Since the purpose of the contest was to give students public speaking experience, she could get that no matter which essay she used, right? Yes, Velvalea decided. She would ignore Miss Muellenschlader's suggestion. She would present the essay she had written without the forensics teacher's approval.

But wait. She had written that essay specifically for a Black audience. How would white people take it? Would it be too tough for the mostly white student body at North Division High School? What would Miss Muellenschlader think of it?

Milwaukee's North Division High School in the 1920s. This is the building where Velvalea attended high school. North Division High moved to a new building in 1978.

Velvalea started changing the wording and the tone of her essay so it would fit in better with the other students' speeches. She tried several times. But no matter what she did, the revised essay didn't have the same effect as the original. It didn't deliver the message she wanted it to. It didn't stir her soul the way it did when she first wrote it. Finally, with Miss Roberts's blessing, Velvalea decided to perform her original essay without changing a word.

The first phase of the contest was held after school in North Division's large assembly room. The audience was made up mostly of the other contest participants and Miss Muellenschlader. She would serve as the contest judge and select the semifinalists.

Velvalea might have felt nervous, but she did her best. She tried to put her whole heart into the words she had written. When she was done, she felt good about her performance. Even so, she must have felt like a load was lifted off her shoulders as she returned to her seat. She probably breathed a sigh of relief.

After all of the contestants had delivered their speeches, Miss Muellenschlader said she would select a total of sixteen semifinalists and post their names on the school bulletin board the next morning. The semifinalists would give their speeches again the following day in a second round of competition. At that time, Miss Muellenschlader would select two finalists in each category. The finalists would present their speeches in a final round to North Division High's entire student body.

No matter what Velvalea thought of her presentation, she knew all that mattered was what Miss Muellenschlader thought.

Chapter 2

Velvalea Speaks Up

When Velvalea got to school the next morning, she went to see if Miss Muellenschlader had posted her list. She had. Velvalea hung back until the kids crowding around the bulletin board left. She felt self-conscious about anyone seeing her look for her name. When everyone else was gone, she got close enough to the list to see if her name was on it.

No Velvalea Rodgers. Well, she thought, no doubt disappointed, at least she'd had a learning experience.

Later that day, Velvalea's older sister, Yvonne, stopped her in the hallway.

"There's something going on and it concerns you," Yvonne said. "What did you do, honey?"

Velvalea had no idea. The mystery deepened later that day when another Black student confronted her.

"Velvalea," she said, "you know there are just a few of us here, and you're causing a lot of problems for us."

Velvalea remained puzzled until the end of the school day. That's when North Division principal Fred Werner summoned her to his office.

Oh no! What kind of trouble could she be in? She couldn't think of anything except the speech contest. Dread gripped her as she headed for the principal's office. Along the way, she conjured up increasingly scary consequences that might be awaiting her. Would she be suspended? What would she tell her parents? Would they be ordered to Mr. Werner's office too? Her dad would be okay. He was pretty easygoing. Her mother, however, would be more worried.

With tears prickling her eyes, Velvalea entered the principal's office. Oh, how horrible! She walked in to find a more terrifying scene than any she could have imagined. In addition to Mr. Werner, both Miss Muellenschlader and Miss Roberts were sitting there. What had they been saying about her?

Velvalea sat broomstick stiff on the edge of the chair Mr. Werner pointed to. When he started talking, he didn't mention the contest or the teachers. Instead, he asked if she knew why students were circulating a **petition**.

"What petition?" a confused Velvalea asked.

The one started by students who thought she should be a speech contest semifinalist, he explained. Velvalea stared at him, bewildered.

"Do you think you were treated fairly?" Mr. Werner asked.

Questions must have swirled around in Velvalea's head. What did he mean? Treated fairly about what? Miss Muellenschlader telling her she couldn't enter her own essay, or saying she had to give a humorous speech, or not selecting her as a semifinalist?

Miss Muellenschlader had definitely treated her unfairly by saying she couldn't present the kind of speech she wanted

to when other contestants were allowed to. But Mr. Werner hadn't mentioned the fact that she had written her own speech. Did he know? Did he or Miss Muellenschlader think it was too controversial for the contest?

She finally asked Mr. Werner if that was what he meant.

After a long pause, he said, "I'd like to hear your speech."

"You mean right now?" Velvalea asked. She stood up, ready to recite.

"No," he replied. "I mean I think we'll have you give it tomorrow at the semifinals."

In other words, he explained, she could be an additional semifinalist competing in the next round.

Velvalea must have felt a mixture of relief and excitement. Still, she hesitated. Her parents had taught her and her sisters that they shouldn't accept anything they hadn't earned. Had Velvalea truly earned a spot as a semifinalist? If she accepted the principal's offer, would that be fair to the other participants who weren't selected?

"Well," she replied, drawing her words out, "I don't know."

The principal said the fact that she had given a speech Miss Muellenschlader hadn't approved had already bent the rules. Adding her to the semifinals wouldn't be any more unusual.

Velvalea continued to hesitate. She could think it over, Mr. Werner said. Maybe she would like to discuss it with her parents. She could let him know the next morning what she decided to do.

Leaving his office, Velvalea glanced at the two teachers. Miss Muellenschlader glowered like a thundercloud while Miss Roberts beamed rays of sunshine.

Velvalea was near tears. As she gathered her things to go home, she spotted a friendly face. Tybie Safer, one of her best friends, was waiting for her so they could walk home together. Even though Tybie was white and Jewish, she and Velvalea lived in the same neighborhood and had become fast friends when they first met.

As they left the school behind, Velvalea told Tybie what had happened in the principal's office. Walking along sidewalks where kids played hopscotch, tag, and jump rope, Velvalea worried out loud about whether she should compete in the speech contest as a semifinalist. She didn't feel right accepting something she hadn't earned, she said.

She had every right to compete, Tybie insisted. Her presentation had earned that for her.

Velvalea's mind must have been whirling with thoughts of how she would tell her parents about the contest results and the principal's offer. By the time she got home, she found a furious mother and a calmer father. Her sister, Yvonne, was already there and had told them that Velvalea had been eliminated from the contest.

When Velvalea said Mr. Werner had offered to declare her a semifinalist and allow her to participate in the next round of speech presentations, her mother's attitude changed. Instead of being angry, she became indignant. She considered the principal's offer condescending. She said Velvalea should tell him no. Her father, however, said she should accept.

That evening, instead of hanging out with her friends while the grownups in the neighborhood tended to asters and daisies in their yards and visited with neighbors sitting on their front porches, Velvalea thought about what she should do.

By the next morning, her mind was made up. She would give her speech.

That day, Velvalea did well enough to advance to the finals.

The final round of the contest took place in the school auditorium before the entire student body. When it was Velvalea's turn to speak, she stood at the microphone. As she stared at the more than two thousand faces focused on her, waiting for her to begin, Velvalea's brain froze. She couldn't even remember her name, much less her speech! Thankfully, it took a couple of minutes for the noisy students, many cheering and clapping and stamping their feet, to calm down.

After taking a deep breath, Velvalea said, "The title of my speech is 'They Shall Not Pass.'" Instantly, the words lined up and flowed out. Once again, Velvalea spoke from her heart about the discrimination that people of color endured throughout their lives in housing, jobs, education, and more.

The students and teachers in the audience must have sensed her passion. Clearly, they took her message to heart. So did the judges, because Velvalea won the contest! Although she had no way of knowing it then, that experience formed a foundation for Velvalea's perseverance and hope in the years to come.

Chapter 3

"I Want to Be a Lawyer"

Velvalea was born in 1923. Her parents, Thelma and Russell Rodgers, named her after an aunt. When she was a young girl, her parents taught her it was important to be nice to everyone and to share, so Velvalea tried to always be nice and hoped others would treat her the same way. When she was still in grade school, she overheard conversations her parents had that started her thinking about helping people who weren't treated fairly.

Thelma and Russell operated a restaurant and bakery and knew a lot of people. When they invited friends to dinner, they often gathered in the kitchen. Velvalea and her older sister, Yvonne, would hide in the back stairwell of the house and listen.

Civil rights lawyer James Dorsey, one of the few Black attorneys in Milwaukee at the time, frequently attended those dinners. The Rodgers home and the Dorsey law office were a few blocks apart in Bronzeville. Bronzeville was a small community of less than one square mile, on the Near North Side of Milwaukee. Many of Mr. Dorsey's law clients were people of color who had experienced racial discrimination. Some

Velvalea (center) with friends

of them couldn't get jobs because white people wouldn't hire them. Some couldn't get bank loans, even though they had the right qualifications. Some had children who weren't allowed to go to good schools that would help them prepare for higher-paying jobs.

Velvalea loved to hear the lawyer talk.

"He had this beautiful voice, and when he entered the conversation, everyone would stop and listen," Velvalea said. "I thought he was wonderful."

Not only did his strong, deep voice impress her, but the things he said impressed her, too. One day when Velvalea was eight, she and her mother were making cookies—oatmeal raisin, Velvalea's favorite.

"Your sister is going to be a dietician," her mother said. "What do you have in mind?"

"I want to be a lawyer like Mr. Dorsey," Velvalea said. "Can I be a lawyer?"

"Of course you can, honey," her mother replied, her round cheery face looking thoughtful. "But it will be hard because there aren't many women lawyers."

That was in 1931, when only three thousand of the nearly two hundred thousand lawyers in the United States were women. Just twenty-four of those three thousand women were Black.

Okay, Velvalea might have thought. So what if becoming a lawyer would be difficult? She could do it.

She studied hard, got good grades, and kept dreaming of being a lawyer. By the time she was twelve, her dream had become her certainty. She had shown her smarts, ability, and grit at age sixteen when she won the high school speech contest. But by her senior year, Velvalea's dream had dimmed. What about college?

With three daughters—Yvonne, the oldest, Velvalea, and Connie, the youngest—their mother had said they couldn't afford to pay for college.

Then Velvalea entered another contest.

This one, sponsored by the Black Elks Club, was national. It also awarded prizes. First prize for the best essay was a four-year scholarship to the college or university of the winner's choice.

Velvalea wrote a new essay, titled "The Negro and the Constitution," and entered it in the contest. Once again, she won!

The college Velvalea most wanted to attend was Howard University in Washington, DC. Howard was one of the nation's first Historically Black Colleges and Universities. Most of the faculty and student body were Black, and the curriculum included African American studies. Velvalea wanted to take those kinds of courses.

With her scholarship covering tuition and money raised by a Bronzeville businessman for other expenses, Velvalea was set. She and her mother took a train from Milwaukee to Washington, DC, to attend Howard's student and parents orientation weekend. On the final day of the weekend, Thelma said she wanted to see the dormitory, Truth Hall, where Velvalea would live. She also wanted to meet the other residents.

Velvalea knew her mother was protective of her daughters. She had strict rules about the types of people they could associate with. They shouldn't smoke, drink, or be loud or disrespectful. Velvalea felt confident about her dorm mates. All would certainly get her mother's nod of approval. But it turned out that not all of them did. After the tour, Velvalea's mother surprised her by naming several students she should avoid. One smoked. Another spoke to her mother using her first name. Yet another was much too loud.

But Velvalea ignored her mother's warnings. She became close friends with all of them.

At Howard, her friends started calling her Vel. She liked the short, punchy sound of it. From then on she became Vel to everyone. Except her mother.

Vel thrived at Howard. She loved her studies. She loved her instructors and professors. She loved her classmates. She even loved the social life, despite the challenges and temptations. (Vel did not smoke or drink alcohol, even though many of her friends at college did.) She also joined the historically Black Delta Sigma Theta sorority, which influenced her lifelong public service. Although Howard provided a safe and inclusive home for Vel, discrimination wasn't far away.

One Sunday morning, a Howard schoolmate suggested they go see the cherry blossoms. Spring had bloomed in Washington, DC, and so had the thousands of cherry trees surrounding the Tidal Basin along the National Mall. Vel felt enthralled by the sight and aroma as they strolled. It made her feel close to God, she said.

"Let's go to church!" her friend exclaimed.

So, they did—only to have their bliss crushed. When they entered the sanctuary of a nearby church, the minister stopped his sermon in midsentence. Caught in the glare of everyone staring at them, the girls froze. The pastor directed ushers to escort them out. That church in the nation's capital was for white people only.

This is not as it should be, Vel thought outside the church's closed doors. But rather than let the pastor and his whites-only church beat her down, the racism she experienced once again lit a fire in her and became another defining point in her life.

Chapter 4

Law School and a Lifelong Partnership

After graduating from Howard University in 1946, Vel returned to Milwaukee. Her dream of becoming a lawyer was as strong as ever, but she wouldn't travel the road alone. Vel's journey toward that goal would soon lead to a lifelong partnership.

Before she could become a licensed lawyer, Vel would need to earn a law degree. To do that, Vel had to answer two questions: Which law school should she attend, and what would it cost? If she were to stay in Wisconsin, she had few options for a law school. It would have to be Marquette University in Milwaukee or the University of Wisconsin in Madison.

As for how to pay for it, she didn't have a scholarship like she had for Howard. Tuition at the state school in Madison was considerably less than at Marquette, which was a private university. But she could live at home while attending Marquette and avoid the housing and other expenses she would have in Madison.

While considering those options, Vel became reacquainted with Milwaukee and its social life. That led her to meet the man who would become the love of her life. Within a few weeks they were married, although no one knew it.

Vel and Dale had noticed each other at a party. They were both certainly eye-catching. Vel's almost perfectly oval face featured gently sloping eyebrows and large compassionate eyes that drew people in. With a hint of dimples in his cheeks, Dale sported a dashing mustache and an easy smile. After Dale asked Vel what her name was, they fell into conversation.

Vel couldn't stop thinking about him. When she got home, she told her mother.

"I met a young man, Mom, at the party, and I was just drawn to him." Vel added that if she got to know him better and still felt that way, she might marry him.

Thelma sat up straight, fanned herself, and said, "What do you mean? You only saw him one time. Oh, Lord Jesus, help me!"

Dale and Vel's law school pictures

A short time after Vel and Dale began dating, they took a quick trip to Iowa and got married. They didn't tell anyone, though, and they continued to live separately.

Dale's charm, good character, and devotion to her won her mother over. He and Vel repeated their wedding vows the following fall in a church ceremony in Milwaukee with family and friends in attendance.

Marrying Dale took care of the question about which law school Vel should attend. It would be UW Law School in Madison. Dale had already completed a year there. Before that, he had served in the US Army during the recently ended World War II. Because of that, he and Vel were eligible to live in Badger Village, a cluster of small homes off campus that served as UW housing for military veterans and their families.

Excitement filled Vel as she began two new phases of her life: attending law school and moving into her and her husband's first shared home.

"It would be the first time we would be by ourselves," she said.

But a petition soon curbed Vel's enthusiasm.

Some Badger Village residents were circulating the petition. It said, "We don't want any Blacks in Badger Village." Vel felt shattered.

Dale knew about racial discrimination and harassment from his time in the army. Enduring that kind of treatment from Badger Village residents would be a distraction, at the least.

"We've gotta get out of here," he told Vel. They moved to a different university housing community and concentrated on their studies and graduating.

Their Badger Village experience was Vel's first taste of the pervasive racial discrimination in housing that Black people faced when trying to find a home to rent or buy. It wasn't just a problem in Madison, either. It happened in cities all over the country, including Vel's hometown of Milwaukee.

Vel's experience at Badger Village wouldn't be her last encounter with housing discrimination. Years later, not only would she and Dale face this type of discrimination again, but Vel would march into a nest of thousands of rabid racists over exactly the same issue.

These homes were part of Badger Village, the University of Wisconsin housing community. This was the location of Vel and Dale's first home as a married couple.

Chapter 5

Bronzeville

When Vel earned her law degree in 1951, she made history. No other Black woman had ever graduated from the University of Wisconsin Law School. Vel's big dream finally came true. She was a lawyer! The same year that Vel received her law degree, she and Dale packed up their belongings in Madison and moved back to Milwaukee.

At the time, graduating from UW Law School and becoming a lawyer were Vel's greatest achievements. But Vel Phillips was just getting started. Next, Vel and Dale opened the law office of Phillips and Phillips in Milwaukee's Bronzeville neighborhood. They planned to specialize in cases related to equality in the workplace, employee compensation, and the legal system.

By the early 1950s, Milwaukee's Black population had grown to more than twenty-two thousand. (It was about fifteen hundred in 1920.) That rapid growth was a result of the Great Migration, which began during World War I. Large numbers of Black Americans started moving from the South to Milwaukee and other northern cities,

Vel enters her and Dale's new law firm around 1951.

Dale and Vel work together in their law office.

hoping to find jobs and better lives. In Milwaukee, the vast majority of those Black residents had been forced to live in Bronzeville, on Milwaukee's North Side. Many white residents didn't want Black people to move into neighborhoods that had always been white. Prejudiced white people feared that would cause their neighborhoods to deteriorate, their property values to decrease, and crime to increase. Thinking they should protect themselves and their property, white Milwaukeeans came up with many ways to keep Black people out of "their" neighborhoods.

Federal and local governments already had enacted **ordinances** (laws passed by local governments), policies, programs, and practices that helped maintain racially

segregated communities. Many of those practices also ensured that the primarily Black North Side neighborhoods would remain in poor condition.

One of those practices was **redlining**. The federal government worked with the Home Owners' Loan Corporation to make maps of American cities, including Milwaukee. The maps were meant to help banks and other organizations decide which hopeful homeowners to lend money to. Neighborhoods on these maps were color-coded according to many factors. Some included the age and condition of the houses. Also included were the race, ethnicity, and religion of the people who lived in those neighborhoods.

    Green areas of the map were in the best condition and populated almost entirely by white people. Those areas were outlined in green. Banks considered it "safe" to lend money to people buying homes in those neighborhoods.

    Red areas of the map were in the poorest condition. Those areas were outlined in red. They were also the neighborhoods where primarily Black residents lived. Banks considered it risky to lend money to people in those neighborhoods. If a resident of a redlined neighborhood wanted to buy or improve a home there, no bank would lend them the money to do so. Even if a resident could buy a home without borrowing money, insurance companies wouldn't sell them property insurance. Ultimately, redlined maps prevented most Black Milwaukeeans from owning their own homes. As a result of this practice, most white residents moved out of redlined neighborhoods and avoided renting or buying homes in them.

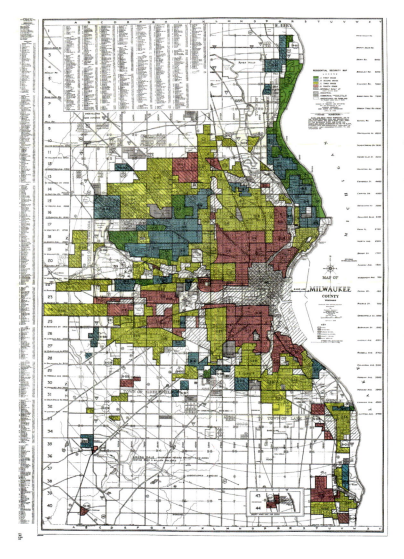

This is a so-called residential security map of Milwaukee County from 1938, created by the US Federal Home Loan Bank Board. Residential security maps were sometimes called redline maps. Black Milwaukee residents were restricted from owning or renting property everywhere in the county except the red sections shown on this map.

Cities also enacted restrictive **zoning** ordinances to create neighborhoods and sometimes even individual blocks that were expensive to live in. Although the ordinances couldn't legally say they were restricted by race, the conditions defined in the ordinances generally applied to Black people.

Another strategy to keep Black people out of white neighborhoods was the use of racially restrictive **covenants**. A racially restrictive covenant is an agreement between people who own property in a neighborhood and people who want to live in that neighborhood not to sell, purchase, or lease homes to Black people. Real estate companies and neighborhood associations supported and **endorsed** these covenants. A property owner who violated a covenant risked losing the property.

Finally, white people who had a home to sell or rent were often racist or afraid to rent or sell to Black people. A Black man Vel would eventually meet, Prentice McKinney, experienced this kind of discrimination firsthand. McKinney's older brother was home from a US Air Force assignment in Europe. He wanted to buy a house in Milwaukee for his family. Wearing his air force uniform, he, his mother, and sixteen-year-old Prentice went to a house displaying a For Sale sign that was well outside the redlined area. When Prentice's brother told the white woman who opened the door that they would like to look at the house, she used a racist expletive to exclaim that she could never sell to a Black person.

Even Vel and Dale, two respected business owners and lawyers, ran into rejection when they tried to move from their second-floor apartment in Bronzeville. White property owners turned them away. According to Vel, "People then could just say, 'We don't rent to you people. We don't sell to you people.'"

All of those factors forced more and more Black residents to live in a one-square-mile area on the city's Near North Side. The Menomonee River valley separated that area from Milwaukee's South Side.

Before most of the city's Black residents found places to live on the Near North Side, that area's population consisted mostly of Jewish people. As the Black population grew, people began to call that area the "Inner Core" or "Bronzeville." Some sneeringly labeled it "Little Africa."

By the time Vel and Dale Phillips opened their law firm, Bronzeville had become a "city within a city." This area was bounded by specific streets. While Bronzeville had some areas that were extremely run-down, it also had thriving businesses, entertainment districts, and community and business leaders.

In addition to building their business with paying clients, Vel volunteered with an organization called the League of Women Voters (LWV). The LWV worked to protect and expand voting rights and ensure all US citizens were represented equally in government. Vel went from door to door in Bronzeville to explain how the city's voting districts were determined and to help residents register to vote.

Some of the homes Vel visited were in poor neighborhoods. That was new territory for her. Although she had grown up in Bronzeville, she had never been to its poorest sections.

"That was my first experience with true poverty," she said, "and my heart just turned over."

This League of Women Voters poster is from 1925, which was just five years after women won the right to vote when the 19th Amendment became part of the US Constitution. Vel was born three years after the 19th Amendment passed.

The houses in Bronzeville were among the oldest in Milwaukee. Some had been built in the mid- to late 1800s. The buildings in the poorest neighborhoods were the most run-down. Many of the landlords who owned them took advantage of their Black tenants by taking their rent money then not spending money on maintenance or repairs. Often the buildings' heating systems or electrical wiring or plumbing didn't work. Some had leaky roofs and crumbling ceilings. The tenants had no power. They had no way to force the landlords to make repairs and they had no options for other places to live.

Vel wished she could do something to help. Eventually, she figured out what that something might be.

By 1955, Milwaukee's population had grown so much that the city had to create a new **aldermanic ward**. That new ward included Bronzeville as well as some white neighborhoods. Next, the people who lived in the new ward would have to elect an **alderman** to represent them in Milwaukee's **city council**, known as the Common Council.

At first, Vel urged Dale to enter the election. He said no.

"Honey, this is not my cup of tea," he told her. "But you have the same credentials I have."

Now *that* was an idea. Should Vel try for the new alderman spot herself? If she did, it wouldn't be her first attempt to win elective office. In 1953, she had run for a position on Milwaukee's Board of Education. In what was becoming her trailblazing way, she had been the first Black candidate to make it past the **nonpartisan**, citywide **primary election**. However, she had narrowly lost the **runoff** and wasn't elected.

The more Vel thought about entering Milwaukee's new aldermanic election, the more intriguing it became. It wouldn't be an easy win, but maybe if she could figure out how to run a successful **campaign**, she might be elected.

This photo was taken when Vel ran for Milwaukee school board in 1953.

Chapter 6

Impossible Odds

Vel faced a huge obstacle to becoming Milwaukee's newest alderman: how would she pay for her campaign? The advertising, flyers, and postage stamps needed for political campaigns cost money, which she and Dale didn't have. Or at least she thought they didn't.

It turned out they did.

For the past few years, Dale had been tucking money away to buy Vel a mink coat, which he knew she wanted. When he told her about his "mink coat fund," it totaled about $3,600. After some discussion, Vel said, "Dale, I'd rather run than have a mink coat. And if it's for me, I should do what I want with it."

Once they settled that question, Vel had to figure out how to organize a successful political campaign. To tackle that, she activated a superpower few people knew she had.

Vel could research.

First, she read a book about how to run for public office. Then she consulted some people she knew. One was former state **legislator** and **county supervisor** Isaac Coggs. He'd been elected to two public offices, so he knew how to run a campaign. The other person she called was Milwaukee newspaper reporter Doyle Getter. Getter had written a story about Vel and Dale being the first married couple admitted to the federal bar in Wisconsin—another historic first for Vel. Being admitted to the federal bar had allowed them to represent clients in the US District Court in Milwaukee.

Vel asked Getter how many women had served on Milwaukee's Common Council. None, he said. When it dawned on him that Vel might run, he tried to discourage her.

"Oh, Vel, I wouldn't do it," he said. "You just wouldn't fit. You're just too dainty. There's a lot of men and they smoke and drink."

Vel didn't see what that had to do with anything.

"Well, I don't have to drink to be a good city council person," she replied.

The more Getter downplayed the notion of Vel running for alderman, the more she wanted to do it. In fact, she thought she might have a good chance of winning, except for two things: One, she was a woman. Two, she was Black.

Being Black shouldn't be a problem, except that the new ward had both Black and white residents. Vel could be pretty sure most, if not all, of the Black voters would choose her. But their votes alone wouldn't be enough to elect her. And some voters might reject her because she was a woman.

But, she wondered, what if voters didn't know she was female? And what if white voters didn't know she was Black? In those days, before social media and when many people didn't have televisions in their homes, political candidates weren't as easily recognized as they are today.

Vel came up with two campaign strategies. One was to change her legal name. Even though she had been known to everyone since college as Vel, Velvalea was still her legal name. If she changed it, her legal name would be Vel on her election filing papers and campaign materials. Unlike the feminine-sounding Velvalea, Vel might be a man's name. In October of 1955, Vel announced her candidacy for the city's new Second Ward. In November, she submitted a request to Milwaukee County to legally change her name from Velvalea to Vel, which was granted.

Her second strategy was to create two sets of campaign materials. One set included her photograph. Those materials were distributed to Black residences. Her picture wasn't on the other set, which her white campaign volunteers distributed in white neighborhoods.

Her strategies seemed to work. An incident on election day showed just how well. Vel and Dale had

A sticker used during Vel's Common Council campaign

volunteered to drive ward residents to their voting places. When Vel asked a white couple who they planned to vote for, the woman said, "Oh, we're voting for Vel Phillips."

"Yeah," her husband added, "we think he's very well qualified."

But before election day, Vel received news that cast doubt on the possibility of her success, no matter how great her qualifications. She was pregnant. Her doctor had called after an appointment to let her know he had something to tell her. Rather than say what it was over the phone, he asked her to come to his office. Vel and Dale had been married for four years, and Vel hadn't gotten pregnant. Their hopes for starting a family had faded. But now . . .

Emotions cascaded over her when her doctor delivered the news. First, relief swept aside her fear that he was going to tell her she had a fatal disease. Then, she was overwhelmed with joy. Speechless shock had set in by the time she returned to the doctor's office waiting room, where Dale was sitting.

Once Dale understood, he was anything but speechless. "Oh, my God, baby," he exclaimed as he hugged her. "What wonderful news!"

Then another thought hit Vel.

Vel and Dale listen to election coverage on the radio.
© Milwaukee Journal Sentinel – USA TODAY NETWORK

Valiant Vel

"Now I'll never win," she said, tears welling in her eyes.

It would have been hard enough for a Black woman to be elected, but a *pregnant* Black woman? In 1956? Impossible.

Vel did the only thing she could think to do. She stowed her maternity news into the same compartment where she kept her gender and race.

After the polls closed on April 3, Vel and Dale awaited results at City Hall, where the ballots were being counted. Sure she wouldn't win, Vel paced the halls as returns came in. Dale finally told her to go home. He would call her when the results were tallied.

When the home phone rang, Dale had the final count.

Vel had won! It had been a five-way race, and Vel had gotten more votes than the four other candidates. Vel's vote count was 1,713. LeRoy J. Simmons came in second place with 1,211 votes.

For the first time in the city's 110-year history, the Milwaukee Common Council had its first Black and first female alderman. With that, Vel Phillips had yet again made history. (Another Black woman, Mary Ellen Shadd, had run for the city's Sixth Ward seat that same year, but she didn't win.)

Vel described her victory as a "double-whammy."

She learned almost immediately after she took office on April 17, 1956, what a "whammy" awaited her. Newspaper reporter Doyle Getter had been right that she wouldn't fit in, but it wasn't because she was too dainty.

Chapter 7

Madam Alderman

From the moment Vel took office in 1956, the other eighteen aldermen on the council shunned, isolated, or scorned her. They did so in ways she expected, and in some ways she didn't. The way she confronted her first challenge was classic Vel Phillips. She took direct action. The problem? Where to go to the bathroom.

Although Vel had been in Milwaukee's City Hall before, she must have been at least a little awed by the grandeur of the Common Council chambers. Ornate chandeliers hung from the high ceiling. Oak desks lined up like rows of individual church pews angled toward a wood-paneled, two-tiered platform. The lower level of the platform held seats for various city administrative officials and a speaker's lectern. The council president's chair sat almost like a throne on the upper tier. A large US flag hung on the wall behind the president's seat.

Intricately carved oak railings separated a couple of rows of spectator benches along the back and on one side of the cathedral-like chamber. Almost within

Vel had a big voice on the Milwaukee Common Council despite the fact that the male council members often disrespected her, ignored her, and refused to take seriously the only female and only Black member of the council.

arm's reach of the back spectator section sat Vel's lone desk, looking just like the add-on that it was.

Vel saw no sign of an important necessity during long council meetings. She soon learned that the closest restroom—or lavatory, as was the common term at the time—was just outside an easy-to-miss door in a back corner of the cavernous chamber. Given that only men had served as aldermen and other city officials, that lavatory was for men only. But now that Vel had won a place on the council, what was she to do? The closest women's restroom was down the hall and around a corner. That wouldn't do. Vel didn't want to miss council discussions every time she needed to take a bathroom break. She knew those trips would become more frequent and urgent as her pregnancy progressed. So, what did she do? Vel used the men's room.

Her male colleagues fumed over what they considered an invasion. Vel didn't apologize. She continued to use the men's room but insisted that she was always respectful.

"I've never walked in on anyone, and I always knocked," she said.

That hardly satisfied the men. One of them had a "Men's *Only*" sign posted on the door. That didn't deter Vel. The men hoped they could cite an existing ordinance that would stop her. But no one could find anything on record that barred women from men's restrooms.

Next came the question of Vel's office. Despite the requirement that aldermen share office space in City Hall, none wanted to be in an office with her. This time, she saw it coming. Common Council President Martin Schreiber broke the news to her. They were afraid, he said, because she was Black and a woman. Vel didn't flinch.

"I want my own office," she shot back. "If they don't want to be with me, I sure as hell don't want to be with them."

So that's what she got, a room she described as the size of a closet with a post in the middle.

Then there was the matter of what to call her. Should she be alderman, alderwoman, alderperson, or something else? After some debate, the council decided on "Madam Alderman." That suited Vel fine. Alderman was the position on the ballot she ran for and that's what her **constituents** had elected. But she did have to wonder, rather than deciding what they thought her title should be, why didn't the men ask her?

The ways her fellow aldermen disrespected her didn't stop with the men's room, office space, or her title. For instance, they didn't include her in the informal conversations they often had behind closed doors, which is how government officials often operate. Instead, they urged her to join the aldermen's wives club. So, she went to a meeting.

"They just talked about baby formula and stuff like that," she said. "It was just unbelievable."

Vel spent the first few years learning everything she could about the ways of the Common Council. How did it function formally? What were the correct terms to use and what did they mean? How did city government relate to other governing bodies and elected officials, such as the mayor, the County Board of Supervisors, and the state **legislature**? How did it work with the state governor? How should she effectively **advocate** for her constituents and their interests? There was so much to know.

All the while, Vel stood up to the other aldermen, but the snubs and insults cut deep. She had expected her new colleagues to exclude her because she was Black. But their sexist behavior surprised and irritated her even more. Generally, she said, white people can eventually accept someone who is Black. "But the men never forget that you are a woman. Never, ever, ever."

Even though she found there were many barriers to her as a woman council member, Vel tackled them, both for herself and for other women. For example, several years after she became an alderman, a group of female City Hall employees asked if she would wear pants to a Common Council meeting. They all wanted to wear pants instead of skirts at work, but their male colleagues and bosses would frown upon it. The women might even be fired. But if Vel led the way, then they would feel they could do it, too. Vel agreed and arrived one morning sporting a conservative, professional-looking pantsuit. At least one newspaper reporter noticed. A short piece ran in the *Milwaukee Sentinel* along with a photograph.

"All 19 aldermen wore pants Tuesday, but the prettiest ones belong to Ald. Vel R. Phillips," the *Sentinel* reported. "The pants were part of a black, all-wool pantsuit— apparently the first ever worn to City Hall by a female city employee or official."

Some members of the public also took note, and not always kindly. One member of the public wrote a critical letter, accusing Vel of "cheapening" herself in front of "thousands and thousands of people who now have no use for you."

Rather than let this racism and sexism distract her, Vel focused on her constituents and their concerns. She handled their complaints about such things as street repairs and signage, crime, traffic, and trash pickup. She also reviewed the problems that Bronzeville renters told her about over and over: electrical, plumbing, heating, and structural problems that didn't get repaired. She soon began to take on broader issues that affected Milwaukee's Black and minority residents outside of her ward as well.

"Being the only Black and the only female member of the council meant that I had to serve more than just those who elected me alderman of the [second] ward, my home district," she said. "I had to represent all African Americans throughout the city and, to a great degree, all the women as well. My fight was their fight, and their fight was my fight."

Vel had a lot to do at home as well. Her first son, Dale Jr., had been born a few months after she became an alderman. At two years old, Dale Jr. got a little brother when Vel and Dale's second child, Michael, arrived.

Vel also found time to work for the Democratic National Committee (DNC). In 1958, two years after she became a Milwaukee alderman, Wisconsin Democratic Party officials elected her to the DNC. That put Vel in the history books yet again. She was the first Black person ever to serve on a major US political party's national committee.

Vel's prominent position in the party gave Democrats a leader who could appeal to Black, female, and Wisconsin voters. Party officials made the most of those qualities. Vel campaigned in Wisconsin with rising Democratic star and presidential candidate US Senator John F. Kennedy.

Kennedy and Vel had become acquainted before he launched his campaign to become president. In a letter he sent her in 1959, he asked her to support **legislation** he, as a

Dale and Vel enjoy a meal with their first son, Dale Jr.

US senator, was sponsoring. He welcomed "any comments you may have, in your capacity as a Democratic leader."

Vel was so enthusiastic that Kennedy might become president, she endorsed him for that office even before he announced publicly that he planned to run.

"Each conversation I have had with Senator Kennedy has increased my feeling that he has the great heart and imagination and the stubborn integrity that are needed to make a great president," she said.

Vel campaigned for Senator Kennedy, joining him at events. Her support for Kennedy contributed to his winning Wisconsin's Democratic primary election in 1960.

Vel also had a key role in shaping the Democratic Party's and presidential-nominee Kennedy's civil rights policy. At the 1960 Democratic National Convention in Los Angeles, Vel and other northern state **delegates** wanted to make a clear pro–civil rights statement. White southern **segregationists**, who made up a large part of the Democratic Party, didn't. One southern senator warned that taking a strong civil rights position could sink Kennedy's and the Democratic Party's chances of winning in that fall's presidential election. Heralding civil rights would cost the Democrats ten southern states, he predicted.

Vel responded, "Winning isn't nearly so important as doing the right thing."

Thanks partly to Vel, the Democrats agreed to the strongest civil rights position in its history. And Kennedy was elected president.

Vel met and became friends with John F. Kennedy when he was a US senator. She supported his successful run for president in 1960.

Chapter 8

Vel's Fight for Fair Housing Begins

During those early years as a Milwaukee alderman, Vel wanted to somehow improve the limited and often terrible housing choices Black people had in the city. Her first effort within the Common Council was to propose the construction of housing projects. She offered plans for apartments, duplexes, and single-family homes, all with low prices and rent. But the other aldermen shot them down.

Vel's experience at the 1960 Democratic Convention and campaigning with John F. Kennedy started her thinking about proposing an ordinance that would lift restrictions on who could live where. An ordinance like that would mean people could live anywhere in the city they could afford, no matter what their color or ethnicity might be.

Vel believed that segregated housing created **segregation** everywhere, including schools and other public facilities, which wasn't allowed by the US Constitution. Cities that were segregated harmed everyone, she thought, not just Black people

Madam Alderman persisted in making herself heard, despite her all-male counterparts' annoyance at having this outspoken Black woman as their peer on the Common Council.

and their communities. An ordinance like the one she had in mind would solve that problem. But it had to be as strong and effective as she could make it. Also, every condition in it had to be within the law and contain no loopholes.

Using her superpower, Vel researched and studied every city, county, and state fair housing (sometimes called open housing) ordinance as well as every national housing law she could find. All of the information she gathered would serve her well when she introduced her ordinance to the Common Council.

On a chilly, overcast Tuesday on the last day of winter in 1962, Vel left her second-floor City Hall office and took the elevator to the Common Council chamber. That day's meeting agenda included Vel's thoroughly researched fair housing ordinance.

Having been an alderman for six years, Vel knew that the council president routinely referred newly introduced ordinances to a committee made up of a small number of council members. The full council seldom voted on it until the committee sent a report with a recommendation. That could be weeks or months later.

Vel's fair housing ordinance went to the council's Committee on Judiciary and Legislation. If that committee made a favorable recommendation and the council approved her ordinance *and* the mayor agreed, all Milwaukee residents would have equal opportunity to buy or rent a home they could afford anywhere in the city.

Vel knew her ordinance wasn't a sure thing. Not everyone liked the idea. Some residents and aldermen strongly opposed it. But no crystal ball could have predicted the six-year battle Vel would face after her ordinance was first presented that day. It would be a battle of conflicting legal opinions involving a volunteer army of kids led by an iconic Catholic priest, all under a national spotlight.

The first obstacle in Vel's battle came when the City Attorney's Office wrote an opinion on Vel's ordinance. That opinion was attached to the Judiciary and Legislation Committee's report. It looked like it might deliver a deadly blow to the ordinance.

"We recognize that the precise question has not yet been passed upon by the Supreme Court of the State of Wisconsin," Milwaukee's assistant city attorney, Ewald L. Moerke Jr., wrote for the City Attorney's Office. "In considering the proposed ordinance, however, we are compelled to judge the powers of the **municipality** on the basis of decisions [the Supreme Court has rendered in other cases]. On the basis of the authorities cited, . . . we must conclude that serious doubt exists as to the power of the Common Council of the City of Milwaukee to enact the ordinance here in question."

The City Attorney's Office was saying that the Wisconsin Supreme Court, which was the highest court in the state, had never stated whether or not cities had the power to enact an ordinance like Vel's. However, based on decisions the court had made on cities' powers in other cases, the city attorney doubted Milwaukee could.

Everyone might have thought the city attorney's opinion put Vel's ordinance on a dead-end road. Everyone but Vel, that is. She knew better. From her research of laws, ordinances, and legal opinions about open housing rules, she understood what cities had the power to do and how city, state, and federal authority related to each other. Her ordinance abided by all existing rules and regulations.

No matter what Vel said, though, no matter what proof she presented, no matter how right she was—none of it made any difference to the other aldermen. When the council voted on Vel's ordinance it went down on an 18–1 vote. Vel alone wanted it.

Such a decisive defeat might have killed any other proposed ordinance, but not Vel's. She was just warming up.

Chapter 9

Obstacles and Opposition

Vel knew Common Council rules would let her reintroduce an ordinance every three months. At first, she vowed to do just that with her fair housing ordinance. But she soon adjusted her plans because of several factors.

One reason was Milwaukee lawyer and civil rights leader Lloyd Barbee. Barbee was already an open housing advocate in 1962 when he moved from Madison, Wisconsin, to Milwaukee. Two years later he was elected to the Wisconsin Legislature. There, he proposed a statewide fair housing law. That same year, Barbee created an organization of civil rights groups and individuals called the Milwaukee United School Integration Committee (MUSIC). MUSIC's mission was to fight segregation in Milwaukee, particularly in schools.

Vel reasoned that if racial segregation could be eliminated in the public school system, that would go a long way toward removing the need for any fair housing ordinance. She also wanted to see if the state passed Barbee's fair housing law. If it did, that too might make an ordinance for Milwaukee unnecessary.

In 1964, civil rights activist, state legislator-elect, and Wisconsin NAACP president Lloyd Barbee walks out of a Milwaukee School Board meeting due to a disagreement over desegregating Milwaukee schools.

Yet another event that affected Vel and the predominantly Black community of Bronzeville during this time was the construction of a highway through Milwaukee. That highway, which became Interstate 43, sliced through the vibrant heart of that "city within a city." Construction—or, rather, destruction—workers bulldozed Bronzeville's booming commercial district to clear a path for the multilane highway and its on- and off-ramps. Demolition crews leveled more than nine thousand homes and businesses.

The tens of thousands of displaced residents and business owners had no other place to live or open a business in the city. Milwaukee government officials had made no relocation plans for the people who lost their homes and businesses.

Private and public restrictions limited Black residents' access to homes almost everywhere in the city except Bronzeville. The thriving city within a city disappeared. Turmoil and uncertainty gripped business owners. People lost their jobs. All of this deeply affected the people of Bronzeville physically, economically, and psychologically.

What alternative was available for these essentially homeless residents, many of whom were also jobless but wanted to stay in Milwaukee? Most of them had to squeeze even more tightly into what remained of their community of Bronzeville. Some moved in with relatives. Others rented rooms or quickly created second-floor or basement apartments.

In the midst of all of that, Vel ran for reelection for the second time as alderman of the Second Ward in 1964. She won with 4,515 votes over her opponent's 2,190. (In 1960, she had won her first reelection 2,723–1,771.)

Vel actively engaged her constituents and kept them informed about the city. One way she did that was over the airwaves. On her *Tell Vel* radio program, she provided informa-

A campaign brochure for Vel's reelection to the Milwaukee Common Council in 1964

tion about job opportunities. She highlighted Black Americans of accomplishment in Milwaukee and elsewhere. She discussed issues at Common Council meetings that were of particular interest to members of minority populations. And, of course, she talked about the city's need for desegregation and a fair housing ordinance.

By 1966, Vel hadn't seen much progress with other Milwaukee desegregation efforts. Barbee's organization had brought about few changes, despite its valiant efforts. His statewide fair housing bill became law in 1965, but it had little effect in Milwaukee because the types of housing it included covered barely a third of the residential units in the city.

Vel had waited long enough. On May 17, 1966, she introduced her fair housing ordinance to the Common Council for the second time. It met the same fate as it had four years earlier. Eighteen aldermen opposed it. Vel alone supported it.

Vel tried a third time the following October and a fourth time in March of 1967. The result never changed. Eighteen against. One in favor.

Each time Vel reintroduced her ordinance, she made changes that she hoped would satisfy some of the objections other aldermen raised. She also tied it to something significant about the date. When her ordinance appeared on the Common Council's May 17, 1966, meeting agenda, she said, "Gentlemen: Today is the 12th anniversary of the 1954 Supreme Court decision (Brown vs. Board of Education) which held that the constitution commanded an end to racial segregation in public schools." While noting the importance of that decision, she said that was but a first step toward equal access.

At the October 12, 1966, Common Council meeting, she began with "Gentlemen, by mere coincidence, the day scheduled for reintroduction of File Number 66-2140 (fair housing) is also the day that Americans have set aside to honor Christopher Columbus." After mentioning the debate over Columbus's discovery of America, she continued, "Historians agree that the first settlers came to our shores in 1620 seeking freedom, freedom in the fullest sense. It is ironic indeed that today, some 346 years later, there still remains a substantial group of American citizens who do not enjoy full freedom." She introduced her March 21, 1967, version with a quote about spring by the German poet and philosopher Goethe and the observation that "today is the first day of spring. . . . and once more the fair housing ordinance." Although she didn't say so, it had been five years and one day since she first introduced her ordinance on March 20, 1962. When the aldermen rejected her most recent version just as they had the previous three, Vel expressed scorn.

"Unless members of this Council have read the cover letter that outlined the two changes, I am positive that the members of this committee are not even aware of what the changes are."

As with previous rejections of her ordinance, Vel promised, "Gentlemen, I will be back."

Vel works with other members of the Common Council.

Obstacles and Opposition

Some versions of the ordinance were introduced at public hearings. Governments can hold public hearings to give citizens an opportunity to say what they think about something the government wants to do. This is one method governments use to gather information about how an official action might affect members of the public.

Vel believed the aldermen in charge of introducing her ordinance at the public hearings might have rigged at least some of them. At one hearing, about twenty-five people and organizations said they liked the ordinance. Only a few said they didn't. When the next hearing was scheduled, Vel learned that most of the people who had been notified about it were community and business leaders who didn't like the ordinance. Only a few people at the previous hearing who had supported the ordinance were notified about the second hearing.

As debate between Vel and the rest of the Common Council raged on, the aldermen and even the mayor dreamed up one objection after another to her ordinance. Alderman Rod Lanser thought the ordinance lacked an enforcement process. It also included types of dwellings he thought shouldn't be included. He thought it should provide more protection for property owners. That included property owners' right to rent or sell to whomever they wished.

Vel knew some of the aldermen personally supported her ordinance, but they voted against it for political reasons. She believed they were afraid voters wouldn't reelect them if they supported it. That was one of the reasons the mayor of Milwaukee, Henry Maier, opposed it. The mayor "flatly told me that my housing bill was causing him 'big problems on the Southside' and costing him votes," Vel said.

Some of the aldermen who resisted the ordinance wanted to keep their districts segregated. Others opposed it because the ordinance might make white people move out of the city. That was called "white flight." If Black people could live in neighborhoods that traditionally had been segregated, the white residents might move to areas outside of Milwaukee's city limits. Milwaukee's fair housing ordinance wouldn't affect them there. They could continue to live in segregated neighborhoods. Vel believed that was another of Mayor Maier's fears. If fewer people lived in the city, then fewer people would pay city taxes. That meant city government would have less money to provide services to residents.

Mayor Maier didn't actually oppose the *intent* of Vel's ordinance to integrate the city's residential areas. In a letter he wrote to the Common Council after Vel introduced her ordinance in September of 1967, he stressed that he believed in everyone's right to live wherever they wanted and the need to "pull down the walls of social segregation between city and suburbs." But he sounded his overriding worry on another occasion when he asked, "How the hell are we going to **finance** a city when the middle class moves out and the needs are here?" Maier wanted an ordinance that applied to all of Milwaukee County, not just the city.

Vel knew that if the City of Milwaukee had less money from taxes, it would hurt all of the city's residents, no matter what their race. But she also knew that neither she nor the mayor had any authority beyond Milwaukee's city limits. Milwaukee County was governed by the county executive and a board of supervisors, not the mayor or the Common Council.

Eventually, Mayor Maier and the rest of the Common Council said they would consider voting for a citywide fair housing ordinance if it were identical to the state's fair housing law. Vel said no. The state law wasn't strong enough, and it didn't include enough types of housing. That would leave too many Black residents in the cold. Also, the consequences for violating the state law were too weak. Plus, she added, what would be the point? A city ordinance that duplicated the state's law wouldn't change anything for Black people and other minorities in Milwaukee. They needed the same kind of access that white people had to better places to live.

Having the Common Council and Milwaukee's mayor against her wasn't going to make things easy. But one thing was for sure—Vel Phillips would not give up.

Then help arrived.

Chapter 10

The NAACP Youth Council Joins the Fight

When Vel met with a Catholic priest in August of 1967, she didn't know it would lead to marching in the streets of Milwaukee with a bunch of Black kids, facing angry white mobs.

The meeting started with a phone call from the priest. Father James Groppi asked Vel if she would meet with him about the fair housing ordinance she wanted the Milwaukee Common Council to approve. He offered to come downtown to her office at City Hall or they could meet at the Freedom House in Bronzeville.

Vel chose the Freedom House.

As a Milwaukee alderman, Vel hadn't worked with the priest directly on city matters, but she knew who he was. She had even met him a couple of times. Once was when he addressed a July 25, 1967, Common Council meeting.

Father James Groppi

At that meeting, Groppi spoke about problems Near North Side residents faced, particularly their housing needs. He warned that city officials' failure to deal with the situation might result in increasingly angry people taking to the streets and rioting.

Groppi, who had working-class roots in Milwaukee, served at St. Boniface Catholic Church, which was located on Milwaukee's Near North Side and had a primarily Black congregation. Promoting social justice and equality had been his mission for most of his adult life. He sympathized with anti-discrimination causes, bonded with like-minded priests, and had participated in civil rights activities in southern cities. He preached about it from his pulpit at St. Boniface, and he talked about it when he taught catechism to the students of St. Boniface Elementary School.

Although he was white, Groppi also served as advisor to the Milwaukee National Association for the Advancement of Colored People (NAACP) Youth Council. Most of the Youth Council members were students in their early to mid-teens who attended St. Boniface Elementary and nearby Roosevelt Junior High.

The Youth Council board members had voted to have their advisor contact Madam Alderman Phillips after Ronald Britton told Groppi about a situation he and his family had experienced. A former US Marine, Britton had recently returned to Milwaukee after serving in the Vietnam War. Accompanied by his wife and baby, he knocked on the door of a house advertising a duplex for rent. They had been unable to find a decent place to live inside the borders of Bronzeville's Black community. Even though the duplex was outside those borders, the Brittons decided to try anyway. The white woman who came to the door said no. She couldn't rent to them, she said. "What would my neighbors think?"

Britton knew about the Youth Council's activism, so he contacted Groppi. When the priest told Youth Council members the ex-Marine's story, they wanted to support him. With the holidays approaching in late 1966, Youth Council members, led by Groppi, gathered at the house of the white woman who wouldn't rent to the Britton family and sang Christmas carols.

That wasn't the first time the Youth Council had used such a tactic to draw attention to racial discrimination in Milwaukee. For months, they had picketed the downtown white-members-only Eagles Club. They also demonstrated and sang freedom songs at the homes of leading city officials and judges who were Eagles Club members. The Youth Council intended to not only spotlight the prejudice but also shame those prominent officials into either resigning from the Eagles Club or resigning from office. The attention they attracted amounted to a few news stories about angry white residents confronting the young demonstrators' invasion of their well-to-do neighborhoods. That only intensified white hostility toward the Black activists instead of highlighting how unfair racial bias was.

Groppi was a constant presence at Youth Council activities and events, including planning meetings, rallies, and pickets. Here, he joins hands and sings with young activists around 1968.

Members of the Milwaukee NAACP Youth Council target downtown Milwaukee's whites-only Eagles Club in 1966. Eagles Club members included Milwaukee city, county, and public school district officials and judges.

With its strategy failing to create change, the Youth Council, with Groppi's guidance, began to broaden its focus and consider other ways to work that might be more effective. That eventually led to the priest's phone call to Vel.

The Freedom House, where Vel had agreed to meet Groppi, was the Youth Council's headquarters and hangout. It blended in with the surrounding one- and two-story frame houses on a quiet, tree-lined Bronzeville residential street. After Vel arrived, Groppi, a slender man with thinning hair and dark-framed glasses, explained that he wanted to meet with her because he thought she and the Youth Council cared about the same thing.

The Youth Council had a security unit of young men called Commandos whose primary job was to keep the younger members safe. Groppi described the Commandos as rough and tumble guys.

"I'm educating them on what it means to do something for their community," he said, "and they really want to help you with your housing issue."

Finally, Vel didn't feel alone. For the past five years she had been fighting a relentless battle to get the city's Common Council to approve her fair housing ordinance. Now, here was this white priest saying that his Youth Council of Black teenagers and Commandos wanted to help her. They would march and demonstrate in support of her fair housing ordinance.

Maybe, just maybe, the Youth Council could be the key to cracking Milwaukee's rigid racism against its Black residents. Vel was willing to try.

"I'll take all the help I can get," Vel told him.

She didn't have to participate in the Youth Council's **demonstrations** or marches unless she wanted to, Groppi said. She didn't say whether she would or not, but the idea intrigued her.

 *Valiant Vel*

SOON AFTER HER MEETING with Groppi, Vel received unexpected visitors.

She had barely returned home from the Freedom House when two men came to her front door. From their dark, conservative-looking suits and swagger that said they were in charge, she figured they were in law enforcement.

She guessed right. "Federal Bureau of Investigation," they said when they introduced themselves. They wanted to talk to her about Father James Groppi. Surprised, Vel invited them into her house and led them to the library. The men were polite and soft-spoken at first. Then their questions became more intrusive. Vel no doubt bristled when she realized they had followed her home from the Freedom House.

They wanted to know what she and Groppi had talked about. Was that their first meeting? If not, when else had they met? What had they discussed? Did she plan to meet with him again? The more demanding and personal their questions became, the more defensive and evasive Vel became. It was her duty as a patriotic American to tell them everything they wanted to know, they said. She needed to do the right thing, they said.

Finally, frustration and the slow burn that had been smoldering inside her flared. Drawing her ninety-three pounds to her full five-foot-one-inch height, Vel stood. They were out of line, she was out of time, and the meeting was over, she said.

After closing the door behind the men, Vel no doubt exhaled with both satisfaction and anger. She hadn't told them anything about her meeting with Groppi, except that it was their first. What did those men expect? That she would be their informant? No way! Not for them or anyone else.

What kind of America do we have here? she thought. She took a deep breath, hoping to slow her racing heart. She knew the country had its warts and that it was governed democratically only as much as the people in power would allow. Lines from the Langston Hughes poem "Let America Be America Again" came to her mind:

The land that never has been yet—
And yet must be—the land where EVERY man is free.

The NAACP Youth Council Joins the Fight

If those agents thought they would intimidate or deter Vel Phillips, they were mistaken. She knew then that she would march with Groppi's Youth Council the first chance she got. As it turned out, Vel didn't get to join in the marches as soon as she would have liked. But she didn't have long to wait.

Chapter 11

Marching for Fairness and Equality

Groppi and the Youth Council's **board of directors** gathered to plan their next action. They discussed ways their campaign against racial discrimination and segregation in Milwaukee might be more effective. Too many people didn't know how prejudice hurt the city's Black residents. Too many others knew very well but chose to ignore it. A lot of people figured that it didn't affect them, so why should they care? The Youth Council leaders wanted to put the city's racism on public display. They wanted to make it harder for them to ignore or deny.

So far, the news media hadn't paid much attention to their protests and demonstrations. If they could get more media coverage, more people might understand and maybe even demand change. So, how could they grab the news media's attention and make bigger headlines? They had to try something different. Something bolder. After tossing around a bunch of ideas, they came up with a plan. Instead of singling out individual establishments and officials, they would target an entire community.

Vel frequently attended NAACP Youth Council meetings and joined members in singing and reciting motivational songs and chants.

"Let's go to the belly of the beast," Commando Prentice McKinney said.

That would be south of the Menomonee River valley. The South Side.

On the evening of August 28, 1967, about a hundred Youth Council members, including Commandos, and other civil rights activists assembled at the north end of the Sixteenth Street **Viaduct**. Their plan was to march to Kosciuszko Park on Milwaukee's white working-class South Side, where they would hold a peaceful **rally**. Many marchers carried signs that read, "We Demand a Fair Housing Bill Covering All Homes," "End Housing Segregation," "We Want Fair Housing," and "Open Housing."

A Milwaukee NAACP Youth Council member carries one of the many signs used in the fair housing marches.

The viaduct started on Milwaukee's Near North Side, a few blocks southwest of Bronzeville. It ran south for about a mile across the Menomonee River Valley to the city's South Side. Below the viaduct's arched supports, on the floor of the valley, lay industrial sites. Those operations included factories, tanneries, construction equipment, and rail yards.

The viaduct ran between the city's North and South Sides. The mostly white South Side included a large ethnic Polish community. That prompted a comedian to joke that the viaduct was "the longest bridge in the world because it connected Africa to Poland."

South Side residents had gotten word that Black people from the North Side were on their way. That night, an estimated five thousand shrieking, angry white **agitators** confronted the Youth Council marchers at the south end of the viaduct. They screamed vile phrases such as "We want slaves" and "Kill, kill, kill." They pelted the marchers with rocks, bricks, dirt clods, and other filth.

Despite the hurled debris and menacing mobs, the marchers reached Kosciuszko Park. They didn't hold a rally as they had planned, though. The noise and press of people were too intense.

Police officers, fearing they couldn't hold the crowd back, told Groppi to pray or do whatever he wanted to do quickly, then get out of there. The marchers didn't know if they would be able to get back through the vicious throngs between them and the viaduct. Many didn't think of anything except putting one foot in front of the other and shielding themselves from the hailstorm of thrown objects.

"We gotta keep moving. We gotta keep moving. We gotta keep moving," college student Margaret "Peggy" Rozga said to herself over and over.

Rozga, who was white, had grown up on the South Side. She knew the streets and how to get around. But misgivings nibbled at her as she marched into her old stomping grounds with a group of primarily Black youths. Although she and the other marchers got back safely, she realized belatedly that she had been terrified.

Marching for Fairness and Equality   69

THE NEXT DAY, Vel had just gotten home from work when the telephone rang. Commando Lawrence Friend, the leader of the Youth Council's security team, told her about a second march planned for that night.

"Oh, I definitely want to be with you," Vel replied. She hadn't been a part of the march the night before.

Friend asked how long it would take her to get there. About half an hour, she said. She had to change her clothes.

"Can you wait?" she asked.

Friend said yes, and they hung up.

"You're going to march?" asked Dale, who had heard Vel's side of the conversation. "Honey, don't you think that could be a little dangerous?" He worried that things would get out of hand. What would happen if the police showed up?

If Vel had misgivings, she didn't share them with Dale. She said she needed to march with the others.

"Honey, this is my ordinance. This is the first time they are marching specifically for my housing bill."

But when she came back downstairs wearing jeans, Dale was nowhere to be found. Maybe he went to the store, their younger son, Michael, suggested. Michael was nine years old by then.

Why would he do that? He knew Vel planned to go out. Surely, he didn't think she would leave their boys home alone. She waited a while for him to return, and then she called her mother, who lived nearby. Could she come over and stay with the boys until Dale got back? Vel asked.

No, her mother replied. In fact, Dale was on his way to her house. He had explained to his mother-in-law that if he wasn't home, Vel wouldn't be able to attend the Youth Council march.

"And I agree with him," Vel's mother said. "It is dangerous."

Also, she added, it wouldn't be ladylike for Vel to be yelling and marching up and down the street.

"Mom, this is wrong!" Vel said, fighting back tears.

Her mother tried to calm her down, but Vel was too angry to talk.

"Mother, I love you, but I'm going to hang up," Vel said.

Later that evening, tears ran down her face as she watched television coverage of what looked like a mob of angry white people confronting and attacking a group of young, orderly marchers. She should have been there.

Next time would be different, she vowed. She *would* be there.

THE YOUTH COUNCIL'S second march pretty much duplicated the first except it involved more of everything—more marchers, more people, more noise, more police, and more violence.

About double the number of Youth Council members and supporters as the night before gathered at the Freedom House. Like the night before, they headed toward the Sixteenth Street Viaduct. This time, Groppi had gotten a county **permit** that would allow the demonstrators to gather at Kosciuszko Park. Still, the previous night provided warning of possible trouble.

At the Sixteenth Street Viaduct the marchers met up with even more civil rights activists and sympathizers. As they crossed the viaduct, they were accompanied by a large police escort and camera crews from the city's three major television stations. Again, a large crowd of screaming white South Siders met them on the other side, shouting obscenities, taunting the marchers, and throwing things. Steely willpower kept the marchers calm, with eyes focused ahead.

Marching for Fairness and Equality

With the possibility of violence growing, the police hauled out guns, tear gas canisters, and gas masks. Even so, they weren't prepared for the surge of more than a thousand agitators at one intersection. With the unarmed Commandos trying to shield the Youth Council teenagers, the mob hit and injured several demonstrators.

Police officers finally managed to herd the procession into a side street. Despite their urging, though, they couldn't discourage the group from continuing its march. At Kosciuszko Park, Youth Council marchers crowded in close so they could hear Groppi speak. Don't hate the tormentors or angry white people, he said as he reminded them of Jesus's teachings. A small explosion cut Groppi off. What was it? A large firecracker? A cherry bomb? No one knew.

Fearing the danger would get worse, Groppi and the Commandos led the others back through the vicious mob toward the viaduct. Later, Vel called the Youth Council's and Commandos' courage "unbelievable."

Although they refused to turn back after the first wave of agitators assaulted them at an intersection, many Youth Council members were scared. "Are we going to make it out of this alive?" one member, Mary Arms, asked herself at the height of the chaos.

Commando Prentice McKinney, a well-built, serious young man, wasn't afraid. He stayed focused on his job. He was there to protect the marchers. Anger surged through him instead of fear. His anger rose with the mob's growing violence against the marchers. No way would those white thugs or anyone else, including the police, intimidate him, even if he went to jail.

When the marchers reached the south end of the viaduct, a small group of police escorted them back to the North Side. That wasn't the end of the uproar, though. Some of the Youth Council's supporters were waiting at the Freedom House for the marchers to return. They got mad when they saw many of the marchers had been injured. They blamed the police for not providing enough protection. They began hurling taunts at the officers and quickly escalated to throwing bottles and rocks at them.

There are different versions of what happened after that.

A number of young marchers had gone inside the Freedom House to rest and

Milwaukee police officers escort Youth Council members and other fair housing supporters as they march past businesses on the city's South Side.

recover from their unnerving experience. As the commotion outside died down, they began to relax. Someone had turned on the TV. They were watching a favorite TV show, *The Fugitive*, when they heard shooting. Scrambling to the windows, they saw only police. Then they realized the house was on fire. They raced out the back door.

Police said they heard gunshots, too, but they didn't know where the shots had come from. They had used tear gas to break up the crowd outside the Freedom House. A tear gas canister must have landed in the Freedom House and set something on fire. Later, police said tear gas didn't start the fire. Instead, they claimed that someone in a passing car had thrown a firebomb at the house and that's what set it ablaze.

No matter what caused the fire, firefighters were delayed getting to it. The reason for this never became clear. One report was that police thought a sniper might be inside and held them off. Later, fire officials said that firefighters couldn't get through key intersections that had been closed during the march and remained blocked afterward as a precaution in case the turmoil continued. Either way, by the time the flames were doused, the Freedom House was beyond repair.

Milwaukee police officers with gas masks pushed up on their heads stand by as the NAACP Youth Council's Freedom House burns.

Chapter 12

These Marchers Won't Back Down

For the second time in less than a month, Milwaukee Mayor Henry Maier imposed restrictions on the city.

The first time, on July 31, 1967, was unrelated to the Youth Council marches. The mayor had put Milwaukee under a round-the-clock curfew, worried that vandalism and violence that had been sparked by a fight in Bronzeville might spread and worsen. Although city officials and white community leaders called the event a riot, it might have been more accurately described as civil disorder or street fighting limited to about fifteen blocks. Whatever it was called—civil disorder, street fighting, or riot—it occurred just three days after Groppi spoke at a Common Council meeting and predicted unrest in response to the poor living conditions of North Siders.

It started late Sunday, July 30, with a fight of some sort outside a nightspot on Third Street. Accounts from Black and white perspectives differed as to whether the fight involved a couple of women or some young people. Police and city officials claimed that the excited onlookers attacked police officers as they began to break things up. Black witnesses insisted that as police got rough with them in the July heat, their frustrations erupted over their wretched living conditions, which included inferior schools and housing, lousy job opportunities, restricted rights, and police harassment and brutality.

As acts of vandalism, arson, and sporadic gunfire broke out and moved down the street, police notified the mayor. Maier put in a call to the governor, Warren Knowles, who arranged to send in National Guard troops to assist Milwaukee law enforcement.

The one thousand officers that Milwaukee Police Chief Harold Brier had ordered to the scene, as well as rain, had cleared the streets. That prompted Brier to report "Everything quiet" by 4 a.m. on Monday. Even so, the mayor blanketed the entire city with a ten-day, twenty-four-hour curfew. He also ordered National Guard troops and police to seal off about 1.5 by 2.5 square miles of the affected area. When it was all over, authorities reported four fatalities, more than a hundred injuries, and nearly eighteen hundred arrests.

Maier, a good-looking man in a lopsided sort of way with a cleft chin, crinkly eyes, and Elvis-style pompadour, earned praise from some for his quick, decisive action. Others thought he overreacted. He was in his second term as Milwaukee mayor and grew more popular with each reelection. Eventually, he would become the city's longest-serving mayor. With his actions that July, Maier no doubt wanted to head off the kind of violence other cities across the country had recently experienced. During what became known as the "long, hot summer of 1967," so-called race riots erupted in Detroit, Chicago, Atlanta, Birmingham, and New York. A couple of those cities suffered double-digit fatalities and costly property damage.

Black Americans everywhere had struggled for more than a decade in what became known as the Civil Rights Movement. They wanted the same access as white people to decent housing, education, and public facilities. Being confined to inferior and inadequate accommodations and services prevented them from asserting their rights as citizens of the United States.

Civil rights activists organized a number of nonviolent events in the 1950s and 1960s. **Boycotts**, sit-ins, and marches, primarily in southern cities, were frequently attacked by violent racists. Many of these events made national headlines. Some of the most notable incidents included the Montgomery, Alabama, bus boycott of 1955; the Greensboro, North Carolina, lunch-counter sit-in of 1960; and the 1965 Selma, Alabama, march across the Pettus Bridge, which became known as Bloody Sunday.

Mayor Maier's curfew made plenty of people mad. It was July. They didn't want to stay inside, especially on hot summer days and nights. After a couple of days,

Dr. Martin Luther King Jr. and his wife, Coretta Scott King (both center), join other civil rights activists on the March 9, 1965, march from Selma to Montgomery, Alabama. The march was intended to support Black citizens' right to vote without interference.

Maier cut the curfew from twenty-four hours a day to nighttime hours only. Then he lifted it completely.

After the Youth Council marches and the Freedom House fire, Maier tried a different strategy. This time, he didn't declare a curfew. Instead, he banned marches and demonstrations in public areas of the city from 4 p.m. to 9 a.m.

Groppi and the Youth Council's board met the next morning. Okay, they said. No marching and no demonstrations didn't mean people couldn't get together. They invited Youth Council members and open housing supporters to a rally that evening at the Freedom House. The Freedom House was private property, so the mayor's ban didn't include that.

Vel was among several hundred people who gathered in the charred house. Despite the stench of burned furniture and stale smoke surrounding them, more and more Youth Council members and supporters crowded in. When more showed up, they stood outside, on the weakened porch and in the debris-littered yard. Then the overflow spilled into a neighboring vacant lot. That was all private property, so no problem.

But still more supporters arrived, and the crowd spread onto the sidewalk and street. That might have meant trouble. As public property, sidewalks and streets came under the mayor's ban. The Youth Council went ahead with its rally anyway. Just as Commando McKinney started to introduce Vel, the police moved in. They ordered everyone to leave and began arresting anyone who resisted.

"What the hell is going on?" Vel demanded, as police chased young people down the street and herded them into patrol wagons. "This is absolutely unbelievable.... I thought we'd be able to have a peaceful meeting."

Still, the Youth Council was not deterred. Groppi called Vel the next day to invite her to another rally that evening at St. Boniface Church.

"Wild horses couldn't keep me away!" she exclaimed.

That night, Vel joined more than four hundred activists at St. Boniface. Everyone applauded and cheered Groppi when he criticized the mayor and his ban. As they became increasingly energized, Groppi asked if they were ready to march. A thunderous "Yeah!" went up. To Vel's surprise and delight, a couple of Commandos hoisted her up on their shoulders.

When they set out, they had a different destination than on the two previous marches. On those occasions, they had marched to Kosciuszko Park on Milwaukee's South Side, where they rallied for open housing. That night, they headed toward City Hall to protest Mayor Maier and the ban that restricted their freedom of movement and right to assemble.

But they never made it.

The marchers had gone only a few blocks when police stopped them. The officers started arresting marchers. They chased and grabbed those who tried to run and hustled everyone into patrol wagons. Amid the uproar, police officers shouted out orders and sometimes even offensive names.

Vel was one of the first of the 137 people who were arrested that night. She felt more disgusted and offended than scared as officers patted her down and loaded her into a patrol wagon with other marchers.

Pamela Jo Sargent, a seventh grader at St. Boniface, was also among those police had rounded up. She was a tiny slip of a thing, barely four feet tall and seventy-five pounds. Because of her size, she managed to slither out of the patrol wagon while others were being herded in. Officers caught her and put her back in. She sneaked out again and was caught again. After a couple more attempted escapes, an officer shoved her far into the wagon and closed the door.

On the ride to the police station, some of the young people looked calm. Others gazed around, wide-eyed. Several murmured or chatted with each other.

No one knew what to expect.

At Milwaukee's District 1 Station, police herded them into holding cells. Thirty to forty kids and adults ended up together in each cell. As the teens chatted among themselves, the Commandos checked around, asking if they were okay.

Finally, guards began taking them to a booking room where officers questioned them individually and in small groups. As parents and NAACP representatives arrived and paid fines of twenty-five dollars per person, the marchers were released and allowed to go home.

It was early morning by the time Dale and a friend came to get Vel, who had been jailed for most of the night. Dale might have been too relieved to tell her

"I told you so." Not so, her mother. Thelma huffed about being embarrassed that Vel had been in jail.

"What will I tell my friends?" she asked.

"Mom," Vel replied, "just tell your friends that your daughter is doing what she thinks is best for her capacity as a member of the Milwaukee Common Council."

Vel continued to do what she thought best. She marched again the next night and began to develop a reputation for being brave and tough.

Chapter 13

"Nobody Is Free Until Everybody Is Free"

On September 19, 1967, after more than two weeks of daily Youth Council marches, Vel brought a fifth version of her fair housing ordinance to the Common Council.

Once again, the other aldermen insisted that Milwaukee didn't have authority to pass its own fair housing ordinance. Once again, the city attorney backed up their claim. Once again, Vel tried to set them straight. Wisconsin state law said exactly the opposite, she told the aldermen. She quoted the Wisconsin attorney general, who was the state's top lawyer. He had stated what Wisconsin's fair housing law did and what cities' authority was.

"It is my opinion that cities, villages, and towns possess the power . . . to promulgate [enact] local regulations to prevent and remove all discrimination in housing," Wisconsin Attorney General Bronson La Follette wrote in his October 3, 1966, opinion.

Milwaukee's two major newspapers had figured that out, Vel added.

"Even giving the City Attorney's office the benefit of the doubt on the matter of integrity, both newspapers concluded that the [city attorney's] opinion is hogwash," she said.

Vel pointed out again that her ordinance would do exactly what the state law authorized and urged Milwaukee to do.

That didn't matter to Vel's fellow aldermen. They all shrugged her off and voted the same way they had the four previous times she had introduced her ordinance. Eighteen against. Only Vel supported it.

This time, an exasperated Vel didn't hold back when she told the other aldermen what she thought.

"I can only say one thing," Vel said. "That either you don't read, and you are not sufficiently knowledgeable to speak to the subject, and that could well be—or you're just afraid to speak, you lack the courage to speak."

Vel then referred to her "rough and tumble" street allies, some of whom sat behind her in the council chamber's spectator section.

"It's quite apparent to me that the members of this honorable body, to put it in the terms of my Commando friends, these cats are just too dumb, too dumb to know when they've got something going for them. It's bad enough to have to deal with a **bigot**, but when you've got a dumb bigot . . ."

Applause and cheers erupted from Youth Council members and Groppi. The aldermen sat in stony silence, many with their arms crossed, staring straight ahead.

Vel concluded by telling her fellow Common Council members that they were out of excuses. "Nobody is free until everybody is free," she said. "And we intend to march, all of us, until we get some of the basic freedoms [t]hat are ours."

Despite her tough talk, when Vel got home that day, she did what she had done after other wrenching defeats. She had a good cry.

Chapter 14

"This Is My Work"

Although a few disillusioned members of the Youth Council gave up after the latest defeat of the fair housing ordinance, most doubled down. They had a cause, and they were going to fight for it. They believed that winning would make the world better. Some were so committed that they defied their elders. When parents or guardians said they couldn't go to the marches, they went anyway.

Sixteen-year-old Gwen Moore had learned about the marches and the fair housing protests from her relative, Prentice McKinney. Disobeying her mother's order not to participate, Moore climbed out of her bedroom window after dark and caught up with the marchers.

That's what Pam Sargent, who was only twelve, did, too. She knew in her heart she was doing the right thing and vowed to march for as long as it took.

"That's what [Groppi] taught in church," Pam said. "He taught us in catechism that it's our duty to right what's wrong."

Pam felt fearless and didn't think about the danger. Then she got hit in the head.

Each night as the Youth Council and other fair housing advocates marched across the Sixteenth Street Viaduct, the Commandos did their job. They repeatedly asked the younger demonstrators if they were okay. The marchers responded with confident nods, smiles, and high fives. They knew the Commandos would protect them.

But the Commandos were no match for the jeering, obscenity-screaming, rock-and-bottle-throwing mob waiting one night at the south end of the viaduct.

Pam didn't see the brick before it hit her. Suddenly, she was on the ground, bleeding. Commando Tommy Lee Woods tore off his shirt and wrapped it around her head to stanch the blood. Even though she had only a flesh wound, several marchers urged her to turn back. Pam refused. Yes, getting hit had been scary, but it also made her mad and more committed than ever. She continued on with the others toward Kosciuszko Park. When the battered marchers returned to safety, another marcher took Pam to an emergency room for stitches.

Some people changed their minds about the marches when they heard that children had been hurt. At first, Pam's grandmother didn't want her to participate in the fair housing protests. But children being injured for standing up for what they believed in wasn't right. She stopped opposing Pam's commitment to protest. Although her grandmother didn't join the marchers, Pam's aunt did. She was one of the adults who added to the marchers' numbers.

When Vel learned about the young marchers' injuries, it affected her almost as much as if her own children had been hurt. But rather than acting like a parent to the marchers, Vel seemed more like one of them.

"When Vel showed up, she fit right in," noted Fred Reed, an NAACP Commando. "She wasn't just another adult talking down to them."

The Youth Council members and Commandos gave Vel a sense of belonging. She had been fighting her lonely battle for so long, and she now had this cohesive and committed bunch of young people sharing the struggle.

"We were a close-knit group," she said. They not only drew energy from each other, she explained, "We all looked out for each other."

At first, Commando McKinney didn't understand why Vel was involved in such a controversial issue. What's this well-educated, middle-class woman living

Vel loved the camaraderie, commitment, shared sense of purpose, and joy she found at NAACP Youth Council gatherings.

a comfortable life doing here in this fight for better living conditions and equal opportunity for poor people? he wondered. It didn't take him long to realize that people's first impression of Vel was based on her outer layer. Beneath her sweet, petite façade lurked a gritty, resolute fighter who would not give up when she knew she was right.

McKinney described Vel as a "steel fist in a velvet glove."

That velvet glove had been fashioned by her mother. Thelma Rodgers's rules—that her daughters behave properly and ladylike—had certainly worked on Vel. She could get into places and get along with people when those who acted angry and belligerent couldn't, McKinney said.

The growing movement confirmed to Vel that she was meant to be campaigning for fair housing.

"It was like, this is my work," she said.

Dale had come to realize that, and he served as Vel's most indispensable warrior. While Vel marched and battled City Hall, Dale kept the trains running in their personal lives. He took care of their two sons as well as many of the household chores and errands. He also managed their law firm, representing clients and handling lawsuits. At night, after Vel had showered and washed mob-hurled dirt, raw egg, and other awful things out of her hair, he massaged her sore, tired feet.

In addition to sharing household and child-raising duties and providing aid and comfort to Vel, Dale assisted in other ways. He served as her chief advisor and partner in every aspect of her political, professional, and **civic** lives. After helping her draft important points that needed to be included in a fair housing ordinance, he worked with her on the many revisions. He also urged her to pause in her hectic schedule to take time to relax and think. No doubt, Vel's view of herself as a "quiet force" reflected Dale's solid, steady influence.

"He knew that I loved what I was doing and he wanted me to be happy," Vel said.

Chapter 15

Wanted: Courage

As the Youth Council doubled down in their fight for fair housing, so did their foes. Angry mobs that numbered in the thousands met the marchers with more spiteful displays of hatred and viciousness. South Siders wanted to keep their neighborhoods white. But the way they fought fair housing demonstrators played into Groppi's and the Youth Council leaders' strategy. With the number of marchers growing and their opponents becoming more violent, the marches became major stories in the news. News reports and photographs of clashes between the marchers and bottle- and rock-throwing crowds with screaming, blood-red faces spread across the country. Headlines such as "Strife Bad for City's Image" ran on Milwaukee newspapers' front pages. Editorial writers demanded that the two sides "Call it off."

The news coverage made Milwaukee city and business leaders squirm. They didn't like the negative attention the city was getting. But the Youth Council didn't stop. They kept marching, day after day, even two or three

times on some days. As the fall start of school and other obligations thinned the Youth Council marchers' ranks on weekdays, more adults picked up the banner. Youth Council member Pam Sargent kept on marching despite her school responsibilities.

"We're going to march until hell freezes over!" she vowed one day when a TV camera was rolling.

Her grandmother saw it on the news and made sure Pam got punished. "Not for skipping school," she said, "but for saying 'hell.'"

Support for the marchers grew. Their cause won support from nearby and far away. The Milwaukee NAACP contacted other branches of its organization for support and asked members to travel to Milwaukee, if possible. In addition to local religious leaders, Catholic nuns, priests, and clergy who shared Groppi's social justice philosophy joined the cause and sent letters of encouragement. One letter of support came from a priest in the African country of Tanzania.

Celebrity comedian and social justice activist Dick Gregory showed up several times. He didn't just add a celebrity face. He marched. He also advised and inspired other marchers.

Dr. Martin Luther King Jr. sent a telegram. "You are demonstrating that it is possible to be militant and powerful without destroying life or property," it said.

Baseball great Henry "Hank" Aaron, who had been the Milwaukee

Vel and baseball great Henry "Hank" Aaron became fast friends when he moved from Alabama to Milwaukee to play for the city's professional baseball team. At the time, the team was called the Milwaukee Braves.

Braves star right fielder, also championed Vel and her campaign. He and Vel had been friends since his early days as a new ballplayer in Milwaukee, where he had experienced intense prejudice in his personal and professional lives.

"She and I will always be kindred spirits," Aaron said of Vel. "While I was fighting for equality from the baseball diamond, she was rooting for me. While she marched for justice on the streets of Milwaukee, I cheered her on."

As the marches continued, so did Vel's long battle with City Hall. In remarks Vel prepared for a Common Council meeting, she pointed out Wisconsin's history of pioneering social legislation. She listed a series of state and federal laws dating back to 1867 that guaranteed more rights and access to Black workers and residents.

"And yet, no social legislation has ever encountered the resistance that is thrown up against fair housing legislation," she wrote.

A Milwaukee newspaper picked up on that. In November of 1967, it published an editorial, headlined "Wanted: Courage."

"We are sure that history will record someday that Milwaukee did approve a local open housing ordinance after a period of political cowardice on the part of the aldermen and the mayor," one paragraph of the editorial read.

But the Common Council majority didn't budge.

While Vel's colleagues didn't go for *her* ordinance, they actually passed another fair housing ordinance. Vel alone opposed it.

Just after Thanksgiving in 1967, Milwaukee Alderman Clarence Miller introduced an ordinance that was almost the same as the state's 1965 fair housing law. Vel did her best to weigh the pros and cons of voting for what she knew was the duplication of a state law that she did not believe would solve Milwaukee's segregation problems. Supporting Miller's ordinance might be seen as a show of "good faith" for a fair housing ordinance, even one that simply echoed the state law. Also, after nearly three months of clashes between the fair housing marchers and opponents, supporting the ordinance could "possibly ease tensions and bring forth a cooling off period," Vel reasoned in her remarks to the Common Council.

Conversely, if she voted to approve Miller's ordinance, it would appear as though she were giving in to pressure and giving up on her people.

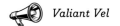 *Valiant Vel*

What she should do depended on the answers to two questions, she said. "First, what have we been fighting for?"

The answer, Vel said, was "for our fair share, for our full measure of freedom." Further, she noted, "during these past few months of marches and demonstrations that have been marked with arrests, taunts and jeers, teargas, fear, the lack of action on the part of this Council has enabled fair housing to become the symbol for all the inequalities that Negroes and other minorities sustain today."

Her second question was, "What will the passage of this ordinance give us?"

Her answer: "Nothing. Nothing, except more of [the] same."

Miller's ordinance, she concluded, "was not what we set out to attain. It is not what we want. It is not what we will settle for. Our aim was not to save face. Our aim was not to take the heat off; our aim was not to win a show of good faith or to achieve a side step instead of a step forward."

Miller's ordinance, Vel concluded, "will not, cannot, satisfy the Black community. The time is here when a few of us will continue to stand firm and strong and tall and to say to you, 'Gentlemen, thanks for nothing but you're too late with too little.'"

Chapter 16

Two Hundred Dangerous Days

The fair housing advocates continued to march. They marched in rain and snow. They marched through the holidays. They bundled up in extra layers of warm clothing and marched in below-zero temperatures on New Year's Eve. They marched on the first day of 1968, when the Green Bay Packers beat the Dallas Cowboys in the infamous Ice Bowl football game.

Vel's Common Council duties and other responsibilities frequently kept her from marching. But when she could join them, she could be found at the front of the group, near Groppi. There, despite her tiny size, she was a bigger target for debris-throwing antagonists than if she had stayed farther back. But she was a leader, she said, so she belonged in front, regardless of the risks.

Vel marveled at the core of people who marched every night, "like clockwork," she said. "Like it was a job."

Having a job—actually, not having a job—became a problem for some of the Commandos. Many had been employed but had lost their jobs because of time

Vel (center) bundles up in multiple layers to march in subzero temperatures with her fellow fair housing activists. © Milwaukee Journal Sentinel – USA TODAY NETWORK

conflicts or because their employers objected to their participation in the marches.

All the while, Vel promoted her fair housing ordinance in a number of ways. She spoke to civic groups, community clubs, and church congregations. She talked to reporters and neighborhood groups. She also fended off critics, often putting them firmly in their place.

For that, she called on her powers of observation and her quick wit. For instance, a fellow alderman referred to the "troublesome" marchers and asked Vel why she didn't "keep her people in line." She pointed to a newspaper with two front-page stories about white men. The man in one story was accused of committing multiple murders. The man in the other story was accused of attempted murder.

"Why don't you keep your people in line?" she replied.

On another occasion, an alderman stopped at Vel's desk in City Hall to tell her he would be voting against her ordinance again because his constituents were against her.

"And I just want you to know that I wouldn't mind having you as a neighbor at all," he said. "That would be fine with me."

Vel must have felt steam blast out of her ears. Like quicksilver, she retorted, "I wouldn't want you to be my neighbor, because neighbors are someone that you can depend on to help you in a crisis."

Later, the alderman apologized and Vel accepted.

At one march, a white man told Vel that the demonstrations were tearing the city apart.

"What is it that you people want?" he asked.

"The same things you want," Vel told him. "Good schools, an opportunity to get a job and to keep it and move forward, a quiet neighborhood, a place for our children to play in. . . . The things that you take for granted and that we don't have."

"Is that it?" the man said, looking surprised. "That's all?"

"That's a great deal if you don't have it," she replied.

Even the mayor tried to put Vel down. Maier often summoned her to his office where he would "read the riot act and swear like a sailor," she said. During one heated conversation, he called her sassy and said that Dale should turn her over his knee and spank her. Imagine how offended she must have felt! That was it, so far as Vel was concerned. She told Maier not to summon her to his office anymore, because she wouldn't go.

As the days and weeks wore on, the Youth Council marches continued to make national headlines. Reporters constantly asked Groppi for information about the ordinance. They wanted to know when the Common Council would be voting on it again and acted as if Groppi were leading Milwaukee's fair housing battle. He always said he didn't know.

"We're just here to support Vel," he said. "You have to ask her."

Some of Vel's allies complained that the priest was getting credit for the ordinance that she had drafted and fought to get approved for more than five years. But since Groppi led the marches and spoke at the rallies, he had become the face of Milwaukee's fair housing fight. Vel understood the situation.

"I don't care who gets the credit," she told a friend who had grumbled to her. "I just want a housing ordinance."

Vel described her role in the movement as legislative. She created "the source of direct action for a fair housing ordinance. But Father Groppi and the [Youth Council] were lightning rods."

"Father Groppi and the Commandos added a drama, a fire, an emotional element," she said.

While the Youth Council's marches attracted media attention, so did Milwaukee government and property association leaders. The news media pointed out that no one in authority stopped police from hassling and arresting the peaceful protestors. They didn't ask why police often turned tear gas on the marchers but not their attackers, or why police arrested people who were being attacked instead of the people attacking them.

How many people showed up to oppose the marches? Estimates went as high as fifteen thousand on some nights. Many opponents armed themselves with sticks, clubs, and projectiles. Those who marched generally numbered in the hundreds on any one night. Their weapons of choice were slogans, songs, and signs.

Groppi became so outraged that the city would not rein in the large crowds of violent antagonists that he asked the governor's office to send National Guard troops to help out. Groppi called the governor, Warren Knowles, only after learning that the Milwaukee police chief and mayor wouldn't. Groppi accused Maier of having a double standard because the mayor had asked Knowles to send National Guard troops during the street violence in July that had lasted only a couple of days and involved a much smaller area and far fewer participants. The governor wasn't available when Groppi called, but an aide turned him down. "We cannot send the National Guard out for just anything," the aide said.

Knowles, who was out of the state at the time, was quoted in news reports as saying "he had offered the National Guard to Maier if he wanted it, but the mayor did not accept the governor's offer."

The increased media coverage of the Youth Council marches had exactly the effect fair housing advocates wanted. That coverage revealed Milwaukee's ugly, racially discriminating underbelly and the city government's hypocrisy.

As the marches grabbed more and more headlines, Vel got more and more hate-spewing phone calls and mail. One letter writer from the North Side complained that Black people were ruining the neighborhoods there. They wanted to stop Black people from buying homes on the North Side, just as the South Side had done.

Some of the messages Vel received went beyond hateful and became threatening. Eventually, things got dangerous not just for her, but for her family as well. One day, a bullet smashed through a window of her house and lodged in the oven door

Milwaukee police try to break up fair housing demonstrations despite Youth Council members' and their fellow activists' determination to remain peaceful.

in the kitchen. Fortunately, no one was home, but someone left a note that said, "Go Back to Africa."

Vel had had it. She and Dale sent their sons to stay with Vel's mom, who was in California at the time. Their younger son, Michael, wanted to know why Vel couldn't come to California, too.

"It was just such a sad time," Vel later said.

On March 14, 1968, the Youth Council brought their marches to an end. They had marched for two hundred days straight and some days more than once. They had yet to decide what they would do next, but the Youth Council leaders and Groppi believed their marching tactic had accomplished all it could.

Chapter 17

A Fair Housing Ordinance at Last

A few weeks after the Youth Council ended its marches, another call to action popped up for Vel. Instead of Milwaukee, this march would take place in Memphis, Tennessee. Instead of fair housing, the cause was workers' rights.

On April 3, Dr. Martin Luther King Jr., with whom Vel had become friends, called to see if she and Groppi would join him in a demonstration for Memphis sanitation workers. The workers were demanding safer and better working conditions. Vel really wanted to go, but she said no.

"I told him I didn't think it would be possible," she said later. "There were big things going on here, too."

King was fatally shot the next day.

Vel felt the shock of King's murder keenly. She had just talked to him the day before. More significantly, she had rejected his request to march with him in Memphis. If she had gone, that would have been the last time she ever would

Civil rights icon Dr. Martin Luther King Jr. sent Vel messages of encouragement and support in her fight for a fair housing ordinance in Milwaukee. Dr. King's work in the South set the example for other nonviolent protests, including Milwaukee's fair housing marches.

have been with him. Had she known that, she wrote later, "perhaps I would have somehow found some way to be there."

At the time, she hadn't noticed the urgency King apparently tried to communicate. She had only asked where he would be going next.

"Vel," King had said, "the time is now. I can only deal with the present and the time is now. I can't think about what's going to be next. I've got to do this now."

Later, she realized that "he had a real sense of urgency, almost a premonition."

Vel couldn't forget that conversation. "He emphasized that he had to do everything right now," she said.

"I cannot put off these important issues," he had told her, "so let's not talk about the next time."

King's words also increased Vel's own need to act now.

"I guess the real moral of the story is never put off for tomorrow what must be done today, and this was true, especially for me as an elected official," she wrote. "And this [is] how I began to view the push for open housing in Milwaukee."

King's assassination sparked violence and rioting in cities across the nation, but not in Milwaukee. While thousands of mourners gathered in the city, the crowd remained largely peaceful. Groppi and the Youth Council's Commandos helped prevent what might have become an explosive situation. Groppi had met with Youth Council members before they joined other civil rights organizations for a memorial march. The priest reminded the youths and young men to "stay cool." The procession had barely begun when a few people began breaking storefront windows. But the mourners shouted "no!" and the Commandos moved in and put a stop to it. As they had during the fair housing marches, the Commandos locked arms and "contained what threatened to become an unruly mob," as city officials said.

Vel said so, too.

"We had grief, we had memorials, we had marches—but we had no death, no violence, no bloodshed," she told Milwaukee's Common Council. "I might also add that Father James Groppi and the NAACP Youth Council are due a great deal of credit for our serenity."

Seven days after Dr. King's murder, President Lyndon B. Johnson signed a federal open housing bill into law. The Federal Fair Housing Act of 1968 was a follow-up to the Federal Civil Rights Act of 1964, which President Johnson had also signed. The 1968 law prohibited discrimination in housing based on race, color, religion, and national origin by landlords, cities, and institutions such as banks. It also prohibited discrimination in zoning and construction, and it outlawed redlining and racially restrictive covenants.

The next day, Milwaukee's mayor announced that he planned to introduce his own citywide open housing ordinance. Mayor Maier, who had previously been opposed to any housing ordinance that applied only to the city of Milwaukee, said he wanted his ordinance to be effective immediately.

"Why wait?" he asked.

Ever watchful for political shenanigans, Vel must have wondered what he could possibly be up to.

Vel had planned to present her latest revised fair housing ordinance at the Common Council meeting scheduled for April 30, 1968. By this time, seven new Milwaukee aldermen had been elected. One of those seven new members was Orville Pitts, who was only the second Black person since Vel's historic 1956 victory to be elected to the Common Council.

To Vel's surprise, the council's April 30 agenda included both her and the mayor's ordinances. At the meeting, Mayor Maier's ordinance went first. But the aldermen took no action. Instead, they delayed voting on it until Vel presented her newly revised draft.

"For the sixth time since 1962, when I first introduced fair housing legislation to this honorable body," Vel told the aldermen, "I come before you and I ask that you act meaningfully, positively, and forthrightly."

As tired as she knew her fellow aldermen were of hearing her talk about fair housing, she was even more tired of talking about it. While she would like to give everyone a break from it, it wasn't up to her, she said.

"Gentlemen, weary, though I am, Black people have been carrying a heavy load for some three-and-one-half centuries, starting with slavery."

Vel speaks in the Common Council chambers around 1970.

When the Common Council voted, Vel's ordinance went down again. But this time she wasn't the only supporter. This time, the result was twelve to seven. That was a far better showing than the previous five defeats. But that wasn't the end of the story.

Instead of swallowing disappointment and bracing herself to try yet again to get her ordinance passed, Vel offered two amendments to Maier's proposal. One

A Fair Housing Ordinance at Last

eliminated a couple of exemptions. The other expanded the amount of Milwaukee's housing that the ordinance would cover from 80 percent to 90 percent. When the council voted on the amendments, nine aldermen voted yes. Ten said no.

Then, in an unexpected twist, one of the aldermen said he wanted to switch his vote. That flipped the total and gave Vel's amendments a ten-to-nine win. The council voted on Maier's proposed ordinance with Vel's amendments. The final count was fifteen for and four against. The Milwaukee Common Council had just passed a citywide fair housing ordinance!

"I think it's a pretty great day for the city," Vel said after the meeting.

Chapter 18

"Victory Is Always Possible"

Although Vel had known she would never stop working to win a fair housing ordinance for her city, she could hardly believe it had finally passed.

"Of course, it was just mindboggling when it happened," she said. "It was wonderful."

Equally amazing was the significant role a bunch of teenagers had played in the victory. The Youth Council members' endurance and dedication also boggled Vel's mind.

"I don't think anyone thought that we would be marching every single day for nearly a year," she said. "I thought we would march for a few days, then I would introduce the ordinance again . . . and if it did not pass within a week or two, they would march again."

How long they would march wasn't on Pam Sargent's mind either. Neither did she think they might be setting a record. She knew she was doing what was right.

Vel rallies with NAACP Youth Council advisor Father James Groppi and Youth Council members atop the repurposed school bus they used for transportation.

Commando Prentice McKinney had lived and marched one day at a time. Doing something historic had never been on his mind.

"We didn't know we were marching into history," he said. "We didn't say, 'We march 200 days and gonna accomplish something.' No, it was, 'We're marching today.' We just knew there was a fight and we were willing to take that fight because it was righteous."

So, why did the ordinance pass on April 30, 1968, after six years and six attempts from one Madam Alderman and thousands of fair housing advocates marching for two hundred days? What made the difference on April 30?

One factor was the relentless driving force of Vel Phillips. She wore the Common Council down. After the April 30 Common Council meeting, Vel said, "I told them that if they didn't do this now, they would be met with it at the next council meeting, and the next, and the next—and I was prepared to carry on through a long, hot summer and the longest, hottest winter this snowy community has ever known."

Two aldermen told a newspaper reporter that they voted for her amendments "to get Vel off our backs."

Other factors helped push the ordinance to victory as well. One was Father James Groppi, the Youth Council, and the attention their marches gave to Milwaukee's need for an ordinance that would ensure Black residents would have equal access to housing in the city. Another was the fact that the makeup of Milwaukee's Common Council had changed. Seven new aldermen had been elected since the first time Vel introduced her ordinance. In addition, enactment of a federal fair housing law led the way for local governments to have similar statutes in their laws. Finally, the assassination of Dr. Martin Luther King Jr. also played a major role. King was a nationally known figure who had died fighting for equality.

Although Vel was overjoyed at the victory in Milwaukee, she was too much of a realist to think that a fair housing ordinance would change the racial map of the city's housing overnight.

"[T]hey say it ain't over until the fat lady sings," Vel said. "She's standing up but she hasn't opened her mouth yet."

Milwaukee's progress in desegregating housing reminded her of the NAACP

Waltz, which she described as, "Two steps forward, a side step and one step backward, which means, of course, that you haven't gone real far."

Many of her young fellow marchers were equally realistic.

Commando McKinney considered Milwaukee's new fair housing ordinance a qualified victory. He didn't celebrate when the Common Council approved it.

"It was the end of one battle and the beginning of another," he said. "If you want to change anything, you have to change the law. But even if you change the law, that doesn't change hearts." McKinney viewed the fair housing ordinance win as "just a stepping stone. . . . [A]s long as you stay this color, you're going to have a fight on your hands."

Youth Council member Peggy Rozga also didn't expect overnight changes. Rozga grew up with social-justice-minded parents and had participated in civil rights activities in the South before the Milwaukee NAACP Youth Council fair housing marches. She knew Milwaukee's new ordinance wouldn't bring immediate changes to the city's residential neighborhoods. But it did begin to establish a legal framework for prohibiting racial discrimination. She also praised the young Youth Council members. "The teens did have the tools and sophistication to carry through [with their cause]," she said.

The bigger victory for Commando Fred Reed was how the marches brought his fellow NAACP Commandos and the Youth Council together and taught them that there were ways to accomplish difficult things. He felt as if their marches had set a precedent.

"We became a family," he said. "We ate together, played together, sang together. We never got tired."

US Representative Gwen Moore certainly saw the passage of Milwaukee's fair housing ordinance as a victory. Moore was sixteen in 1967 and early 1968 when she disobeyed her mother by climbing out of a window to join the marchers. Like Vel Phillips, Moore won a high school speech contest. She continued to achieve astonishing things. Because of her fair housing activism as a teenager, housing became a priority in her own public service as a Wisconsin and US legislator.

Moore once described Vel as "the one who walked through the valley of the

shadow of death over and over again to bring justice and social justice to her people."

Still, Milwaukee's fair housing victory was but one step toward the overall goal of equal access and opportunity. "Every generation has to work on it," Moore said.

In the years after the hard-fought fair housing ordinance became law, Vel understood how deeply she had been affected by the North Division High School speech contest and the teacher who tried to bar her from delivering her own essay.

"Throughout all of the battles and struggles that African Americans experience in Milwaukee and across America over fair housing law, police brutality, employment discrimination, or whatever else," Vel wrote in the prologue to an autobiography she would never complete, "I always turn to that one single event in my life as a reminder that whatever we face, whatever we endure, whatever the odds, victory is always possible."

Epilogue

Winning a fair housing ordinance for Milwaukee wasn't the end of Vel Phillips's story.

Vel served as alderman and Milwaukee Common Council member for fifteen years. Then in 1971, Wisconsin's governor, Patrick Lucey, appointed her to serve as a judge on the Milwaukee County Children's Court. When Vel took her oath of office to serve as a Wisconsin judicial officer, she became the first female judge and the first Black judge in Milwaukee County. She also became the first Black judge in the entire state. Although she loved being a juvenile court judge, Vel lost the election for a full term in 1972. She returned to practicing law with her husband, Dale.

A few years later, Vel saw another opportunity to serve the public. She entered the 1978 election for Wisconsin secretary of state, and she won! That win placed Vel in the history books once again. She was the first Black person ever elected to a statewide **executive office** in Wisconsin. She was also the first Black woman ever elected to statewide executive office in the country. She ran for reelection in 1982 but didn't win.

No longer serving in public office gave Vel and Dale more time to spend together. They traveled to Nevada where their son, Michael, lived with his new family. They

Secretary of State Phillips at her desk in 1979

became acquainted with their first grandchild. But a few years later, the possibility of serving in public office beckoned once again.

In 1988, a US House of Representatives seat in Vel's congressional district became available. She considered running for it. She believed that serving in public office was the best way she could help people.

"[I felt] that making a difference in the world, that's all I really wanted, to make a small difference," she said.

Dale encouraged her.

"Honey," Vel remembered him saying, "you'd be perfect for it."

Then disaster struck. Dale, her greatest love and partner in everything she did, suffered a fatal heart attack. Vel never fully recovered from the loss. She chose not to run for Congress.

As she worked through her grief, Vel settled into teaching law and supporting civic groups and charitable causes. She also established a foundation that provided college scholarships and other opportunities to disadvantaged youth.

Vel and Dale in 1982

Vel reengaged with public service by acting as a mentor to her longtime friend and fellow fair housing marcher Gwen Moore. Moore had been a member of the Wisconsin State Assembly and the state Senate since 1988. When she decided to run for an open seat in the US House of Representatives in 2004, Vel exclaimed, "Gwen, we're going to have so much fun!"

Moore had always admired Vel's cheerful optimism, tenacity, fearlessness, and class blindness.

"The money you had in your pocket, the state of your hair, and the shoes on your feet didn't matter to Vel." Moore wrote in a remembrance three weeks after Vel died at age ninety-five on April 17, 2018. "What mattered was that you envisioned a better future for our city."

Despite Vel's joy over the passage of Milwaukee's fair housing ordinance, it didn't solve the city's segregation problems. Large numbers of white Milwaukee residents moved to suburbs with less restrictive fair housing laws. Unfortunately, a sort of "jobs flight" followed. Numerous businesses and manufacturers relocated their operations to suburban communities. That left Milwaukee's Black residents with fewer and fewer decent-paying jobs in the city.

Nevertheless, Vel Phillips's fight for fair housing made a difference. It forced many to confront the city's racism. Her grace, persistence, and courage have made her an inspiration to many.

Vel has become one of the state's most celebrated and highly regarded citizens. That's clear from the numerous places that bear her name, which include:

- A residence hall at the University of Wisconsin–Madison
- The Milwaukee County Vel R. Phillips Juvenile Justice Center, formerly the Milwaukee County Children's Court
- The Milwaukee Common Council Chamber Vel R. Phillips anteroom in the Milwaukee City Hall
- The Vel R. Phillips Plaza in downtown Milwaukee
- Vel Phillips Memorial High School in Madison
- Vel Phillips Middle School in Oshkosh

In addition, a sculpture of Vel Phillips stands on the Capitol Square in Madison. This posthumous honor catapults Vel into another rare place in US history. Fewer than 7 percent of the 5,193 public statues in the United States are of women. Vel's sculpture is also the only representation of a Black woman to stand on state capitol grounds, nationwide.

Vel's legacy continues to live on in other ways. Among her many activities, she participated in monthly meetings of a group called the Community-Brainstorming Conference. Reserve Judge Russell Stamper, who once chaired the conference, remembered her as being as active as any twenty-five-year-old person he knew.

"Vel," Stamper observed, "is past, present, and future."

Vel's sculpture went up near the Wisconsin State Capitol building in the summer of 2024.

Afterword

In the fall of 1967, I was nine years old. My brother, Dale, was eleven. On Saturday mornings we watched cartoons, plopped down in our pajamas before our new color TV set. One Saturday morning, we heard a commotion coming from the front of the house. Voices shouting. The noise was coming from our front porch. Dale and I moved a chair from the library to the front door, climbed up, and looked out of the one-way glass built into the upper part of the door. We were surprised to see a crowd of heads and shoulders on our front porch! We agreed, however, that the shouting voice was our mother's. We got down from the chair and began arguing about what to do. I got scared and, before my brother could stop me, I opened the front door.

A squad of burly Black men turned toward us, faces scowling. I had never seen such big people. They towered above us, seeming to take up even the air. But they parted suddenly, and I saw my parents standing in the middle of them, looking no bigger than children themselves. We ran to my father, who looked down upon my brother and me with his steady smile—the one that had warmed me my whole life—and I knew then that everything was okay. He looked out from the porch, and I followed his gaze.

Afterword

Only then did I see the crowd. Thousands of people filled every crevice of our street, all standing and looking up at my mother. For Mom had a bullhorn and she was talking about "fairness" and "rights." Things I didn't yet understand. But I knew, somehow, that she was safe. I gathered that the big guys were there to guard her, protect her. And everything changed. One of the big guys looked down and gave me a crooked smile. He was big and beautiful. My father led my brother and me back into the house, and we watched from the front window as the fair housing march unwound from our front porch.

So much has changed since that moment almost sixty years ago. My parents and my brother are gone. The house is gone. But the freedoms that my mother fought for and the rights she marched for—those issues remain current in American society.

I am reminded of something my father used to say. "Mike," he would counsel, "as an adult, you'll be a citizen of your city, your county, your state, your nation, and of this world. Do your best to understand your responsibilities to each of those. Step into the shoes of your fellows and walk around. Imagine them as people just like you and do your best to understand the hard facts of their lives. Then work to make all our lives better and vote accordingly."

My father's good advice still lives in me today. It always will.

Michael Phillips
March 2024

Author's Note

During introductions at a 2003 women's peace symposium, Vel Phillips gave only her name to those of us sharing a table. She seemed more interested in hearing about me and the six other attendees we sat with than talking about herself.

I learned later that Vel Phillips had been a judge, Wisconsin's secretary of state, and a Milwaukee city alderman. She made history when she attained each of those positions. But she first made history in 1951 when she graduated from the University of Wisconsin Law School.

Wanting to know more about this trailblazer, I looked for a book about her. I couldn't find one. Amazing! Vel Phillips changed the face of Wisconsin's prestigious law school, Milwaukee's Common Council, the state and county judiciary, and statewide elective office. Why had no one written a book about her? The newspaper, magazine, and journal articles I found contained the basics about her, but little of her origin story. Where and how had she grown up? Who and what had influenced her? Where did her drive, determination, and perseverance come from?

After several years of waiting and watching, I saw no indication that anyone was writing Vel Phillips's biography. Okay, then. I would. A biography for young people, whom I hoped would find Vel's life story inspiring.

Before that happened, Vel died. She was ninety-five.

Even though I already knew a lot about her from the articles I had read, I wanted to know *her*. I contacted her son, Michael Phillips. He needed to know my plan, and I hoped he would help.

I understood from some of Vel's and my mutual acquaintances that she had been writing her autobiography but hadn't finished before she died. When I first called Michael, he didn't have it and didn't know where it was, but he promised he would let me know if he found it. He eventually located the prologue of her autobiography, but nothing more. Later, I found Chapter 1 and the book's outline in the University of Wisconsin–Milwaukee Libraries Archives' Vel Phillips Special Collection. Much of the information in this book, including nearly all of the first few chapters that detail Vel's experience during the high school speech contest and how she decided to become a lawyer, comes from that prologue, the first chapter, and the chapter outline.

Although at times I have speculated about what Vel might have been thinking, I have not invented any of the direct quotes or details in the story. Vel included much of that in the prologue and first chapter of her unpublished autobiography, which she had titled *A Dream Deferred*. I also read a great deal of her unpublished writings in the Vel Phillips Special Collection.

My research also included conversations with Michael, a relative he suggested, and other people who had known Vel well. In addition, I scoured the internet for information about her, read books that mentioned her, and contacted several historical societies. Those and other sources I found especially useful include:

- The PBS Wisconsin documentary *Vel Phillips: Dream Big Dreams*
- Wisconsin Black Historical Society and Museum
- Vel Phillips Special Collection, archived by the Wisconsin Historical Society at the University of Wisconsin–Milwaukee Libraries Archives
- A Marquette University history class presentation transcript
- Several *Milwaukee Journal Sentinel* newspaper and other periodical articles
- *The Selma of the North: Civil Rights Insurgency in Milwaukee*, a book by Patrick D. Jones
- *City with a Chance: A Case History of Civil Rights Revolution*, a book by Frank A. Aukofer
- *Two Hundred Nights and One Day*, a book in verse by Margaret Rozga

Acknowledgments

So many people and institutions helped with the creation and publication of *Valiant Vel: Vel Phillips and the Fight for Fairness and Equality*, it is impossible to acknowledge everyone. With apologies for any oversights, the following were most instrumental.

Michael Phillips, whose invaluable assistance, advice, trust, and encouragement helped make *Valiant Vel* a reality and bring his mother, Vel Phillips, to life in its pages.

Wisconsin Black Historical Society and Museum founder and director **Clayborn Benson**; America's Black Holocaust Museum staff, especially former head griot, historian, educator, writer, and public speaker **Reggie Jackson**; UWM Library Archives staff; Milwaukee's Municipal Research Center staff **Eileen Lipinski** and **Kathleen Williams**, and Milwaukee County Historical Society Archivist **Steve Schaffer**.

Others who shared memories, information, and insights include:

- **Margaret Rozga**, former Milwaukee NAACP Youth Council member, 2018 Wisconsin Poet Laureate, author, essayist, educator, widow of James Groppi
- **Dr. Sandra E. Jones**, educator, community champion, author of *Voices of Milwaukee Bronzeville*

- **Reuben Harpole**, civil rights and community advocate and "unofficial Mayor of Milwaukee"
- Vel's close friend and mentee, **US Congresswoman Gwen Moore**
- Former NAACP Youth Council members and Commandos **Pamela Sargent**, **Fred Reed**, and **Prentice McKinney**

Thanks, also, to Marquette University researcher, program coordinator, and faculty **Benjamin Linzy** whose invaluable work saved me time, hassles, and stress.

My eternal gratitude to my dear friend, writing buddy, author, and essayist **Jill Giencke** (a.k.a. Kate Fellowes), for her shoulder, ear, expertise, encouragement, and for always being there. Also, to my uber critique partner and all-around confidant **Sandy Brehl**; insightful critique partner, writing instructor, and book promotion/marketing innovator **Rochelle Melander**, and other SCBWI-WI critique group members.

Thank you, Wisconsin Historical Society Press Acquisitions Editor **Kate Thompson**, for believing in me and opening the WHS Press door.

WHS Press Senior Editor **Maria Parrott-Ryan**, my dream editor, whose expertise, insight, and patience guided *Valiant Vel* into this most excellent book.

My deepest gratitude to my family for their understanding and support, and most importantly to my husband, **Hibbie**, for his patience, forbearance, and faith in me, who journeyed with me despite more than two years of debilitating and life-threatening health issues.

Glossary

advocate: (noun) A person who defends, supports, or promotes a cause or group; (verb) To support or argue for a cause or group
agitator: A person who stirs up public feeling on controversial issues
alderman: Someone elected to represent the people in city government
aldermanic ward: A division of a city in which an alderman is the representative
board of directors: A group of people who manage or direct a company or organization
bigot: A person who won't listen to beliefs other than their own, and especially one who treats members of a racial group with hatred and intolerance

Glossary

boycott: To refuse to have dealings with a person, store, organization, or group in an attempt to force its acceptance of certain conditions

campaign: A connected series of operations meant to bring about a particular result; can apply to advertising, politics, the military, social justice, and other fields

city council: A group of people that makes laws for a city

civic: Relating to citizenship, a city, or a community

civil rights: The rights of personal freedom guaranteed to US citizens by the Constitution and acts of Congress

constituents: The residents in an electoral district

county supervisor: A person who makes laws for a county

covenant: A written agreement or promise between two or more individuals or groups

delegate: A representative to a convention, such as that of a political party

demonstration: A public display of group feelings toward a person or cause

endorsed: Approved or recommended

executive office: A job or position within the executive branch of government

finance: To raise or provide money for

forensics: An educational program that allows students to participate in speech and debate competitions

legislation: The laws and statutes passed by a state or national legislature

legislator: A person who makes laws as a member of a legislature

legislature: An elected group of people who have the power to make laws for a state or nation

municipality: A self-governing city or town

nonpartisan: Not supporting or representing the ideas of any political party

oratory: Public speaking that uses familiar expressions and appeals to the emotions

ordinance: A law passed by a local (city, county, village, or town) government

permit: A written statement of permission from someone in authority

petition: A written request for change signed by people in support of a shared cause or concern

primary election: An election in which voters choose their party's candidate for an upcoming general election

rally: A meeting meant to stir a group's enthusiasm

redlining: A strategy used to discriminate against a group of people in housing or insurance

runoff: A final election to decide an earlier one that did not result in victory for any of the possible candidates

segregation: When referring to race, the separation of people based on racial identity

segregationist: A person in favor of segregation, especially segregation based on race

viaduct: A bridge built for carrying a road or railroad over something, such as a highway or river

zoning: The act of separating a city or town into zones reserved for different purposes

Bibliography

BOOKS

Aukofer, Frank A. *City with a Chance: A Case History of Civil Rights Revolution.* Milwaukee: Marquette University Press, 2007.

Black, Ivory Abena. *Bronzeville: A Milwaukee Lifestyle; A Historical Overview.* Milwaukee: The Publishers Group, 2008.

Geenen, Paul H. *Civil Rights Activism in Milwaukee: South Side Struggles in the '60s and '70s.* Charleston, SC: The History Press, 2014.

Geenan, Paul H. *Milwaukee's Bronzeville, 1900–1950.* Charleston, SC: Arcadia Publishing, 2006.

Jones, Patrick D. *The Selma of the North: Civil Rights Insurgency in Milwaukee.* Cambridge, MA: Harvard University Press, 2009.

Jones, Sandra E. *Voices of Milwaukee Bronzeville.* Charleston, SC: The History Press, 2021.

Rozga, Margaret. *Two Hundred Nights and One Day.* Hopkins, MN: Benu Press, 2009.

Trotter, William Joe, Jr. *Black Milwaukee: The Making of an Industrial Proletariat.* 2nd ed. Urbana: University of Illinois, 2007.

Phillips, Vel. *A Dream Deferred: Vel Phillips and the Long Journey of Wisconsin's Civil Rights Movement.* With Leonard Sykes Jr. Partial unpublished autobiography.

DOCUMENTARY

Trondson, Robert. *Vel Phillips: Dream Big Dreams.* PBS Wisconsin Documentaries. Milwaukee, 2015. 56:45. Video. www.pbs.org/video/wpt-documentaries-vel-phillips-dream-big-dreams.

PRIMARY SOURCE DOCUMENTS

Vel Phillips Special Collection, Wisconsin Historical Society, University of Wisconsin–Milwaukee, UWM Libraries, Archives.

MAGAZINES, NEWSPAPERS, AND OTHER PERIODICALS

Nye, Abigail. "Undaunted Persistence: The Extraordinary Life of Vel Phillips." UWM Libraries Archives. Story Maps, Summer 2020. https://storymaps.arcgis.com/stories/35c9312bae00426aaf3348146af1f232.

Miner, Barbara. "Valiant Lady Vel: Phillips Was a Major Figure in City's History." *Milwaukee Magazine,* April 19, 2018.

Sandomir, Richard. "Vel Phillips, Housing Rights Champion in the '60s, is Dead at 95." *New York Times,* April 25, 2018.

ORAL HISTORY INTERVIEWS
Mary Arms, interviewed by Amanda Wynn, March on Milwaukee Civil Rights History Project, UWM Libraries/WHS, July 29, 2007.
Pam O'Halloran, interviewed by Michael A. Gordon, March on Milwaukee Civil Rights History Project, UWM Libraries/WHS, August 16, 2007.
Margaret "Peggy" Rozga, interviewed by Michael A. Gordon, March on Milwaukee Civil Rights History Project, UWM Libraries/WHS, June 19, 2007, July 29, 2007, August 19, 2008.

INTERVIEWS BY THE AUTHOR
Clayborn Benson, Wisconsin Black Historical Society and Museum founder/director, in person in Milwaukee, Wisconsin, August 20, 2022.
Adam Carr, social justice activist, March on Milwaukee 50th Anniversary event organizer, in person in Milwaukee, Wisconsin, October 31, 2022.
Shaune Curry, Vel Phillips's niece, by telephone, May 2019.
Reuben Harpole, Milwaukee's "second mayor," civil rights and education advocate, Bronzeville and Milwaukee Black community historian, community organizer and developer, academic and foundation executive, in person in Milwaukee, Wisconsin, October 28, 2022.
Sandra Jones, PhD, University of Wisconsin–Milwaukee professor of English, African and African diaspora studies, author, in person in Milwaukee, Wisconsin, November 28, 2022.
Prentice McKinney, Milwaukee NAACP Youth Council Commando, by telephone, February 18, 2023.
Gwen Moore, fair housing marcher, Vel Phillips's mentee and friend, US congresswoman, by telephone, February 17, 2023.
Michael Phillips, Vel Phillips's son, in person in Milwaukee, Wisconsin, February 19, 2019, June 4, 2019, by telephone and email on numerous other occasions.
Fred Reed, Milwaukee NAACP Youth Council Commando and Vel Phillips's longtime assistant/driver, in person in Milwaukee, Wisconsin, September 19, 2022, October 6, 2022, by email, March 27, 2023, by telephone, March 29, 2023.
Margaret Rozga, Milwaukee NAACP Youth Council Member, essayist, poet, widow of Milwaukee NAACP Youth Council advisor James Groppi, in person in Milwaukee, Wisconsin September 29, 2022.
Pamela Jo Sargent, Milwaukee NAACP Youth Council member, by telephone October 3, 2022, November 2, 2022, February 13, 2023.

Source Notes

CHAPTERS 1 AND 2
All quotations: Phillips, *A Dream Deferred.*

CHAPTER 3
14 "He had this beautiful voice . . .": Alexander Gelfand, "Women in Law: Six UW Trailblazers," *Gargoyle: Alumni Magazine of the University of Wisconsin Law School,* June 16, 2018.
14 "Your sister is going . . ." to ". . . there aren't many women lawyers.": Miner, "Valiant Lady Vel," 5.
17 "Let's go to church!": Trondson, *Vel Phillips: Dream Big Dreams.*
17 This is not as it should be: Trondson, *Vel Phillips: Dream Big Dreams.*

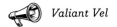

CHAPTER 4
All quotations: Trondson, *Vel Phillips: Dream Big Dreams.*

CHAPTER 5
27 "People then could just say...": Jones, *The Selma of the North,* 176.
28 "That was my first experience...": Miner, "Valiant Lady Vel," 6.
29 "Honey, this is not...": Miner, "Valiant Lady Vel," 6.

CHAPTER 6
30 "Dale, I'd rather run...": Miner, "Valiant Lady Vel," 6.
31 "Oh, Vel, I wouldn't..." to "Well, I don't have to...": Trondson, *Vel Phillips: Dream Big Dreams.*
32 "Yeah, we think...": Trondson, *Vel Phillips: Dream Big Dreams.*
32 "Oh, my God, baby...": Trondson, *Vel Phillips: Dream Big Dreams.*
34 "Now, I'll never win": Trondson, *Vel Phillips: Dream Big Dreams.*
34 "double-whammy": WPR Staff, "Wisconsin Civil Rights Leader Vel Phillips Dies at Age 94," wpr.org, April 18, 2018, www.wpr.org/wisconsin-civil-rights-leader-vel-phillips-dies-age-94.

CHAPTER 7
38 "I've never walked in on anyone...": Miner, "Valiant Lady Vel," 7.
38 "I want my own office...": Trondson, *Vel Phillips: Dream Big Dreams.*
39 "They just talked about...": Trondson, *Vel Phillips: Dream Big Dreams.*
39 "But the men never forget...": Miner, "Valiant Lady Vel," 15.
39 "All 19 aldermen wore pants...": Lainey Seyler, "Everything You Want to Know About Vel Phillips That's Probably Not in a History Book: She Wore Pantsuits," *Milwaukee Journal Sentinel,* April 18, 2018.
39 "cheapening... thousands and thousands...": Nye, "Undaunted Persistence."
40 "Being the only Black and the only female member...": Nye, "Undaunted Persistence."
42 "any comments...": US Senator John F. Kennedy to Vel Phillips, letter, July 20, 1959. Vel Phillips Special Collection, UWM Libraries Archives.
42 "Each conversation I have had...": Seyler, "Everything You Want to Know."
43 "Winning isn't nearly...": Sandomir, "Vel Phillips, Housing Rights Champion."

CHAPTER 8
46 "We recognize that the precise question...": Ewald L. Moerke Jr., memo, Milwaukee's Office of the City Attorney, Milwaukee Common Council proceedings, April 23, 1962.

Source Notes   129

CHAPTER 9

53 "Gentlemen: Today is the 12th anniversary . . . ": Vel Phillips, Communications from City Departments, Milwaukee Common Council proceedings, May 17, 1966, 357.

53 "Historians agree that the first settlers . . . ": Vel Phillips, Communications from City Departments, Milwaukee Common Council proceedings, October 18, 1966, 1531.

54 "Today is the first day of spring . . . ": Vel Phillips, Communications from City Departments, Milwaukee Common Council proceedings, March 21, 1967, 2796.

54 "Unless members of this Council . . . ": Vel Phillips, Communications from City Departments, Milwaukee Common Council proceedings, March 21, 1967.

54 "Gentlemen, I will be back.": Nye, "Undaunted Persistence."

55 "flatly told me that my housing bill . . . ": Phillips, *A Dream Deferred.*

56 "pull down the walls . . . ": Milwaukee Mayor Henry Maier to Vel Phillips, letter, September 9, 1967, Municipal Research Library, Milwaukee.

CHAPTER 10

58 "What would my neighbors think?": Margaret Rozga, "March on Milwaukee," *Wisconsin Magazine of History* 90, no. 4 (Summer 2007): 28–39.

61 "I'm educating them . . . ": Phillips, *A Dream Deferred.*

61 "I'll take all the help I can get": Phillips, *A Dream Deferred.*

62 What kind of America . . .: Phillips, *A Dream Deferred.*

CHAPTER 11

65 "Let's go to the belly of the beast": Trondson, *Vel Phillips: Dream Big Dreams.*

67 "the longest bridge in the world . . . ": Jones, *The Selma of the North,* 1.

67 "We want slaves . . . ": Margaret "Peggy" Rozga, interview, March on Milwaukee Civil Rights History Project, UWM Libraries/WHS, June 19, 2007.

67 "We gotta keep moving . . . ": Rozga, interview.

69 "Honey, this is my ordinance . . . ": Phillips, *A Dream Deferred.*

70 "And I agree . . . " to "I'm going to hang up": Phillips, *A Dream Deferred.*

71 "Are we going to make it out of this alive?": Mary Arms, interview, March on Milwaukee Civil Rights History Project, UWM Libraries/WHS, July 29, 2007.

CHAPTER 12

75 "Everything quiet": William Dahik, "Civil Disorder of 1967," *Encyclopedia of Milwaukee,* http://emke.uwm.edu/civil-disorder-of-1967.

77 "What the hell . . . " to " . . . have a peaceful meeting": Aukofer, *City with a Chance,* 161.

77 "Wild horses couldn't . . . ": Phillips, *A Dream Deferred.*

79 "What will I tell . . . " to "Milwaukee Common Council": Trondson, *Vel Phillips: Dream Big Dreams.*

CHAPTER 13

80 "It is my opinion that cities . . .": Phillips, draft Common Council remarks, Vel Phillips Special Collection, UWM Libraries Archives.

82 "Even giving the City Attorney's office . . .": Phillips, draft remarks, 5. Vel Phillips Special Collection, UWM Libraries Archives.

82 "I can only say one thing . . .": Sandomir, "Vel Phillips, Housing Rights Champion."

82 "It's quite apparent . . .": Trondson, *Vel Phillips: Dream Big Dreams.*

82 "Nobody is free . . .": Aisha Turner, "NAACP Commando Prentice McKinney Looks Back at Milwaukee's Open Housing Marches, 50 Years Later," *Lake Effect,* WUWM 89.7 FM, August 28, 2017, 6:44.

CHAPTER 14

83 "That's what [Groppi] taught in church . . .": Pamela Jo Sargent, interview by the author, November 2, 2022.

84 "When Vel showed up . . .': Fred Reed, interview by the author, October 6, 2022.

84 "We were a close-knit group . . .": Trondson, *Vel Phillips: Dream Big Dreams.*

87 "It was like, this is my work": Trondson, *Vel Phillips: Dream Big Dreams.*

87 "He knew that I loved . . .': Trondson, *Vel Phillips: Dream Big Dreams.*

CHAPTER 15

90 "We're going to march . . .": to ". . . for saying 'hell.'": Sargent, interview.

90 "You are demonstrating . . .": Margaret Rozga, "Moving Forward on Fair Housing," *Milwaukee Neighborhood News,* April 2, 2017, https://milwaukeenns.org/2018/04/02/moving-forward-on-fair-housing/.

91 "She and I will always be kindred spirits . . .": Henry "Hank" Aaron, Vel Phillips Foundation website, About Vel Phillips, accessed June 16, 2018, www.velphillipsfoundation.com/vel.htm.

91 "And yet, no social legislation . . .": Vel Phillips, draft Common Council remarks, Vel Phillips Special Collection, UWM Libraries Archives.

91 "We are sure that history will record . . .": Phillips, *A Dream Deferred.*

91–92: "possibly ease tensions . . ." to ". . . 'you're too late with too little.'": Vel Phillips, draft remarks. Vel Phillips Special Collection, UWM Libraries Archives.

CHAPTER 16

93 "like clockwork": Trondson, *Vel Phillips: Dream Big Dreams.*

94 "Why don't you keep . . .": Miner, "Valiant Lady Vel," 10.

94 "and I just want you to know . . ." to "in a crisis": Vel Phillips, presentation to Marquette University History 191 (Technology for Historians) students, John P. Raynor, S.J., Library, April 28, 2008, 15–16. Vel Phillips Special Collection, UWM Libraries Archives.

95 "What is it . . ." to ". . . if you don't have it.": Trondson, *Vel Phillips: Dream Big Dreams.*

Source Notes 131

95 "read the riot act . . .": Miner, "Valiant Lady Vel," 16.

95 "We're just here to support . . .": Phillips, presentation to Marquette University History 191.

95 "the source of direct action for a fair housing ordinance . . .": Nye, "Undaunted Persistence."

95 "Father Groppi and the Commandos . . .": Phillips, _A Dream Deferred._

96 "We cannot send the National Guard . . .": Rozga, "March on Milwaukee," 28–39.

96 "he had offered . . .": Rozga, "March on Milwaukee."

97 "It was such a sad time . . .": Phillips, _A Dream Deferred._

CHAPTER 17

98 "I told him I didn't think . . .": Phillips, _A Dream Deferred._

100 "Vel, the time is now . . ." to ". . . the push for open housing in Milwaukee": Phillips, _A Dream Deferred._

100 "We had grief, we had memorials . . .": Phillips, draft remarks. Vel Phillips Special Collection, UWM Libraries Archives.

101 "Why wait?": Chris Foran, "Milwaukee Gets a Strong Open-Housing Law, a Surprise to All but the Woman Who Fought for It," _Milwaukee Journal Sentinel,_ April 24, 2018, Updated April 25, 2018.

101 "For the sixth time . . .": Phillips, draft remarks. Vel Phillips Special Collection, UWM Libraries Archives.

101 "Gentleman, weary though I am . . .": Phillips, draft remarks. Vel Phillips Special Collection, UWM Libraries Archives.

103 "I think it's a pretty great day . . .": Sandomir, "Vel Phillips, Housing Rights Champion."

CHAPTER 18

104 "Of course, it was just mindboggling . . .": Trondson, _Vel Phillips: Dream Big Dreams._

104 "I don't think anyone thought . . ." Phillips, _A Dream Deferred._

106 "We didn't know we were marching . . .": Dylan Deprey, "March on Milwaukee 50th Anniversary Inspires 200 Nights of Freedom Initiative," _Milwaukee Courier,_ September 2, 2017.

106 "I told them that if they didn't do this now . . ." to "get Vel off our backs": Foran, "Milwaukee Gets a Strong Open-housing Law."

106 "[T]hey say it ain't over . . .": Phillips, presentation to Marquette University History 191.

107 "Two steps forward . . .": Miner, "Valiant Lady Vel."

107 "It was the end of one battle . . .": Prentice McKinney, interview by the author, February 18, 2023.

107 "just a stepping stone . . .": Talis Shelbourne, "You Can't Legislate Morality: Nearly 60 Years after Milwaukee's First Stab at Fair Housing Legislation, the City Struggles to Enforce It," _Milwaukee Journal Sentinel,_ February 25, 2022.

107 "The one who walked through the valley . . .": Annysa Johnson, "Vel Phillips Remembered as Pioneering Civil Rights Leader at Memorial Service," _Milwaukee Journal Sentinel,_ May 6, 2018.

109 "Every generation has to work on it": Gwen Moore, interview by the author, February 17, 2023.

109 "Throughout all of the battles . . .": Phillips, _A Dream Deferred._

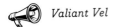 *Valiant Vel*

EPILOGUE
113 "[I felt] that making a difference in the world...": Phillips, presentation to Marquette University History 191.
114 "Gwen, we're going to have so much fun!": Gwen Moore, "Remembering Vel, Our Revolutionary," *Milwaukee Neighborhood News Service,* May 4, 2018.
114 "The money you had...": Moore, "Remembering Vel."
115 "Vel is past, present, and future": Miner, "Valiant Lady Vel."

Index

PLEASE NOTE THAT THE PAGE NUMBERS IN *ITALICS* INDICATE IMAGES.

A

Aaron, Henry "Hank," 90–91, *90*
alderman. *See* Milwaukee Common Council
Arms, Mary, 71

B

Badger Village, 20–21, *20–21*
Barbee, Lloyd, 48, *49*, 53
Board of Education, Milwaukee, 29
Brier, Harold, 75
Britton, Ronald, 58
Bronzeville, 12, 22–23, 27–29, 49–52, 58, 74–75

C

campaigns, for Milwaukee Common Council
    first campaign, 29, 30–34
    re-election campaign, 52
civil rights, 42–43, 48. *See also* fair housing ordinance; Federal Civil Rights Act (1964);
    Federal Fair Housing Act (1968); housing discrimination; marches; Youth Council
    Civil Rights Movement, 75–76
Coggs, Isaac, 31
Commandos, 61, 65, 69, 71, 77–78, 84, 93–94, 100, 106–107
covenants, racially restrictive, 27

D

Delta Sigma Theta sorority, 15
Democratic National Committee (DNC), 40–43
desegregation, 53, 106–107. *See also* fair housing ordinance; segregation
Dorsey, James, 12–14

E

Eagles Club, 58–59, *60*

F

fair housing ordinance. *See also* housing discrimination; marches
    impact of, 114
    marches for, 65–72, *66, 72,* 83–84, *85,* 93–96, *94, 97*
    passage of, 101–103, 104, 106–109
    public opposition to, 88, 96–97
    rejected by Common Council, 45–47, 48, 53–56, 80–82
    supported by Youth Council, 61
    Vel promotes, 91, 94–95
Federal Bureau of Investigation, 62–63
Federal Civil Rights Act (1964), 101
Federal Fair Housing Act (1968), 101
Freedom House, 57, 61, 70, 71–73, *73,* 77
Friend, Lawrence, 69

G

Getter, Doyle, 31, 34
Great Migration, 22–23
Gregory, Dick, 90
Groppi, Father James, *57*
    and assassination of Martin Luther King Jr., 100
    attends Youth Council rallies, 77
    background, 58–59
    and passage of fair housing ordinance, 106
    supports Vel at Common Council, 82
    Vel begins association with, 57–58, 61–63
    with Youth Council, *59, 60, 65, 105*
    and Youth Council marches, 64, 67, 70, 71, *94,* 95, 96, 97

H

House of Representatives, 112–113, 114
housing discrimination, 20–21, 23–27, 44–47. *See also* fair housing ordinance
Howard University, 15

 *Valiant Vel*

I
Interstate 43, 49–52

J
Johnson, Lyndon B., 101

K
Kennedy, John F., 40–43, *43*
King, Coretta Scott, *76*
King, Martin Luther Jr., *76*, 90, 98–100, *99*, 106
Knowles, Warren, 75, 96
Kosciuszko Park, 65–67, 70, 71, 78, 84

L
La Follette, Bronson, 80
Lanser, Rod, 55
League of Women Voters (LWV), 28, *28*
Lucey, Patrick, 111

M
"Madam Alderman," 38
Maier, Henry, 55–56, 74–78, 95, 96, 101–103
marches. *See also* fair housing ordinance
    banning of, 77
    beginning of, 61, 65–67, 70–71
    continuation of, 83–84, 93–94
    end of, 97
    impact of, 107
    news coverage of, 88–90, 96
    opposition to, 77–78, 88, 95–97
    and passage of fair housing ordinance, 104–106
    Vel's participation in, 63, 69–70, 77–79, 84
Marquette University, 18
McKinney, Prentice, 27, 65, 71, 77, 83, 84–85, 106, 107

Miller, Clarence, 91–92
Milwaukee
    Black population of, 22–23
    Bronzeville, 12, 22–23, 27–29, 49–52, 58, 74–75
    housing discrimination in, 23–27
    Near North Side, 12, 27, 58, 67
    restrictions imposed on, 74–75, 76–77
    South Side, 27, 65–67
Milwaukee Common Council
    discrimination in, 36–39
    fair housing ordinance rejected by, 45–47, 53–56, 80–82
    Miller's fair housing ordinance brought before, 91–92
    passes fair housing ordinance, 101–103, 106
    Vel's first campaign for, 29, 30–34
    Vel's re-election campaign for, 52
    Vel's service on, 36–43
Milwaukee County Children's Court, 111
Milwaukee National Association for the Advancement of Colored People (NAACP) Youth Council.
    See Youth Council
Milwaukee Sentinel, 39
Milwaukee United School Integration Committee (MUSIC), 48
Moerke, Ewald L. Jr., 46
Moore, Gwen, 83, 107–109, 114
Muellenschlader, Helen, 1–3, 4, 5, 7–8

N

Near North Side, 12, 27, 58, 67. *See also* Bronzeville
"Negro and the Constitution, The" essay, 14
North Division High School, 1–9, *3*, 109

O

open housing ordinance. *See* fair housing ordinance

P

pants, and City Hall employees, 39
Phillips, Dale Jr., 40, *42*

Phillips, Dale Sr., *19, 23, 33, 113*
 courtship and marriage of, 19–20
 death of, 113
 and fair housing marches, 69–70
 with family, *42*
 racial discrimination experienced by, 20–21
 on running for alderman position, 29
 supports Vel's fight for fair housing, 87
 and Vel's first alderman campaign, 30, 34
Phillips, Michael, 40, 69, 97, 111
Phillips and Phillips law firm, 22
Pitts, Orville, 101
poverty, 28–29
pregnancy, 32–34

R
racial discrimination. *See also* fair housing ordinance; housing discrimination
 experienced by Vel, 2–3, 15–17, 20–21, 27, 38–39, 96–97
 housing ordinance's impact on, 49, 107
 and impact of Interstate 43's construction, 49–52
 in Milwaukee, 23–27
 and Vel's alderman campaign, 31–32
 and Vel's aspirations to become lawyer, 12–14
 and Vel's tenure as alderman, 38
racial stereotypes, 2–3
racially restrictive covenants, 27
redlining, 24–26
Reed, Fred, 84, 107
restroom, for Milwaukee Common Council, 37–38
Roberts, Agnes, 2, 4, 7, 8
Rodgers, Russell, 7, 9, 12–14
Rodgers, Thelma
 and fair housing marches, 69–70
 friends and activism of, 12–14
 impact on Vel's activism, 85
 and speech contest, 7, 9
 on Vel's arrest, 79

Index 139

on Vel's career aspirations, 14
and Vel's college education, 15
on Vel's courtship, 19
Rodgers, Yvonne, 5, 9, 12, 14
Rozga, Margaret "Peggy," 67, 107

S

Safer, Tybie, 8–9
Sargent, Pamela Jo, 78, 83–84, 90, 104
schools, segregation in, 48
Schreiber, Martin, 38
sculpture on state capitol grounds, 115, *115*
Secretary of State, 111, *112*
segregation, 23–26, 44–45, 48, 53, 55–56. *See also* desegregation; fair housing ordinance
sexism, 37–39
Shadd, Mary Ellen, 34
Simmons, LeRoy J., 34
Sixteenth Street Viaduct, 65, 67, 70–71, 84
South Side, 27, 65–67
speech contest
essay selection for, 1–4
impact of, 109
outcome of, 5–9
St. Boniface Church, 77
Stamper, Russell, 115

T

Tell Vell radio program, 52–53
"They Shall Not Pass" essay, 2, 3–4, 9. *See also* speech contest

U

University of Wisconsin Law School, 18, 20–21, 22
US House of Representatives, 112–113, 114

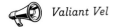 *Valiant Vel*

W
Werner, Fred, 7–8, 9
white flight, 55
Woods, Tommy Lee, 84

Y
Youth Council
    activism of, 58–61, *59, 60, 65, 105*
    arrest of members of, 78
    and assassination of Martin Luther King Jr., 100
    celebrity support for, 90–91
    cheer for Vel before Common Council, 82
    Commandos, 61, 65, 69, 71, 77–78, 84, 93–94, 100, 106–107
    commitment of, 83–84
    impact of, 107
    marches of, 64–73, *66, 72,* 77–78, 83–84, 85, 88–90, 93–94, *94,* 95, 97, *97*
    opposition to, 88, 95–96
    rallies held by, 77
    role in passage of fair housing ordinance, 104–106
    Vel first gets involved with, 61–63

Z
zoning ordinances, 27, 101. *See also* fair housing ordinance

Image Credits

CHAPTER 1

Yearbook photo, Milwaukee County Historical Society. North Division high school, UW–Milwaukee Libraries Thomas and Jean Ross Bliffert Postcard Collection.

CHAPTER 3

Velvalea and friends, courtesy of the Phillips Family Archive.

CHAPTER 4

Vel and Dale law school pictures, UW Law School Digital Archives. Badger Village homes, University of Wisconsin Collection.

CHAPTER 5

Vel enters law office, WHi image ID 119508. Dale and Vel working, WHi image ID 119516. Residential security map, American Geographical Society Library, University of Wisconsin–Milwaukee Libraries. League of Women Voters poster, WHi image ID 37894. Vel portrait, WHi image ID 51783.

CHAPTER 6

Campaign sticker, WHi image ID 120193. Vel and Dale listening to radio, © Milwaukee Journal Sentinel – USA TODAY NETWORK.

CHAPTER 7

Vel and other Common Council members, WHi image ID 119102. Vel, Dale, and son, WHi image ID 119301. Vel and John F. Kennedy, courtesy of the Phillips Family Archive.

CHAPTER 8

Vel in Common Council chamber, WHi image ID 119398.

CHAPTER 9

Lloyd Barbee at school board meeting, WHi image ID 5763. Campaign brochure, WHi image ID 120192. Vel and other Common Council members, WHi image ID 119378.

CHAPTER 10

Groppi portrait, WHi image ID 92286. Groppi and others singing, WHi image ID 5295. Eagles Club protest, WHi image ID 53595.

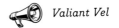 *Valiant Vel*

CHAPTER 11
NAACP Youth Council meeting, WHi image ID 119129. Marchers with signs, WHi image ID 97930. Fair housing marchers with police escort, WHi image ID 94025. Freedom House burning, WHi image ID 48147.

CHAPTER 12
Selma, Alabama march, Abernathy Family via Wikimedia Commons.

CHAPTER 14
Vel and NAACP Youth Council members, WHi image ID 119125.

CHAPTER 15
Hank Aaron, WHi image ID 118397.

CHAPTER 16
Fair housing marchers bundled up, ©Milwaukee Journal Sentinel – USA TODAY NETWORK. Fair housing marchers face off against police, WHi image ID 595547.

CHAPTER 17
Dr. Martin Luther King Jr., Library of Congress, LC-USZ62-126559. Vel speaks in Common Council chambers, WHi image ID 101443.

CHAPTER 18
Vel and Youth Council on school bus, WHi image ID 48149.

EPILOGUE
Secretary of State Phillips, WHi image ID 119265. Vel and Dale, WHi image ID 119281. Vel Phillips sculpture, Maria Parrott-Ryan.

GLOSSARY
Vel riding a bike, WHi Image ID 101435.

BIBLIOGRAPHY
Vel pitching, WHi Image ID 119255.

SOURCE NOTES
Vel giving speech in snow, WHi Image ID 119104. Vel with binoculars, WHi Image ID 118350.

INDEX
Vel walking down the sidewalk with child, WHi Image ID 119284.

About the Author and Contributors

JERRIANNE HAYSLETT is an award-winning journalist, writer, and trial court information officer. She became interested in children's literature when she began reading picture books—and creating them—for the little people in her life. As they grew, she volunteered in their schools. Her reading list grew, too, to middle grade and young adult books. Professionally, Jerrianne has worked as a newspaper reporter and editor and a freelance writer. Her book *Anatomy of a Trial: Public Loss, Lessons Learned from The People vs. O. J. Simpson* was published after she served as media liaison and court communications officer during O. J. Simpson's criminal trial in Los Angeles. She left her native state of Virginia at age nineteen. Jerrianne has lived overseas and in several US states, including Wisconsin, which has been her home for longer than anywhere else.

AARON BOYD knew by age five that he wanted to be an artist. Inspired by artists inside the pages of children's books at his local library, by age six he knew what he wanted to do with his art: make children's books. After graduating from the Milwaukee Institute of Art and Design, Aaron practiced his craft in children's magazines and board games before illustrating his first picture book in 1999. Since then, Aaron has illustrated dozens of books and begun writing and illustrating his own stories. Aaron illustrated *The Story of Civil Rights Hero John Lewis* and the Wisconsin Historical Society Press title *Brownie the War Dog*.

MICHAEL PHILLIPS is the son of Vel and Dale Phillips and administrator and board member of the Vel Phillips Foundation. Michael has spent years serving as an attorney in Madison and Milwaukee.